Life of a Man Named
Kenneth

Kenneth Rogers Bridges

© 2019 by Kenneth Bridges

ISBN 9781790826391

AptWord, Inc.

Printed in the United States of America

Foreword

One of my earliest memories of time spent with "A Man Named Kenneth" was going to cattle shows. It was a unique experience because I was just an elementary school kid and I got to pal around with the high school students who would be on the trip with my uncle — the Agriculture Teacher.

My Uncle Kenneth helped me select my very first show heifer. He is one of the most respected agriculture teachers in Georgia. It was amazing to watch how the students responded to him. It has also been memorable to witness the enthusiasm and charisma this man named Kenneth seems to possess with every activity. No matter if the conversation is regarding hunting dogs, FFA student activities, shorthorn cattle, or his family, my uncle can provide the most energetic and entertaining stories that will warm your spirits and lighten your troubles. Even during the most difficult times, I have witnessed my uncle share his genuine love for others. I truly believe this is one reason so many of his former students speak so fondly of A Man Named Kenneth; because they actually know how much he truly cares about each of them. His life of service is an inspiration.

As a Hall of Fame agriculture education teacher, FFA Advisor, and producer of Shorthorn Cattle, Mr. Kenneth Bridges has been one of the most influential leaders in agriculture. His work is well documented and the fruit of his labor is still actively making a positive difference in the world through the various people he impacted during his professional career.

Equally impactful is the way Kenneth Bridges treats everyone he meets. He always has time for others and makes them feel important. His work ethic is also legendary. I have heard my dad talk about growing up poor and spending long days picking cotton with his brothers. Perhaps the humble upbringing and strong family faith is something that has made my Uncle Kenneth such an inspiring character. The kind of character who truly makes a positive difference in the lives of others. The kind of character that you would be proud to meet. My Uncle Kenneth is the kind of character that you should read about if given the opportunity.

Finally, there is now a book about the *Life of a Man Named Kenneth.*

John (Chip) Bridges
AG Teacher & FFA Advisor
Lumpkin County High School

CONTENTS

"The longer I live, the more I realize the impact of attitude on life. Attitude, to me, is more important than facts. It is more important than the past, than education, than money, than circumstances, than failures, than successes, than what other people think, say, or do. It is more important than appearance, giftedness, or skill. It will make or break a company ... a church ... a home. The remarkable thing is we have a choice every day regarding the attitude we will embrace for that day. We cannot change our past—we cannot change the inevitable. The only thing we can do is play on the one string we have, and that is our attitude. ... I am convinced that life is 10 percent what happens to me and 90 percent how I react to it. And so it is with you ... we are in charge of our attitudes."

—Kenneth Rogers Bridges

Chapter 1

Growing Up

I was born the first of four boys and one girl to Ralph and Lucy Rogers Bridges at my grandfather and grandmother Benjamin and Bethel Gordon Rogers' home at Rogers Mill. I never got to know my Grandfather Ben. He died a year before I was born. However, I know the location of his grave. His dad, William S. Rogers, was born September 13, 1813, and died May 10, 1899. John Rogers III was born October 26, 1789, and died in April 1853. I have in my files three different copies of the Rogers Ancestry and all trace back to John Rogers who came to America on the Mayflower. It states that he was of a goodly sort. John Rogers was born 1588 in Wales, England. He died in December 1674 in the United States. Also, I have in my files the ancestry of my grandmother Bethel Reo Gordon, born December 4, 1885, and died August 2, 1976. She married Ben F. Rogers on May 19, 1906. To this union six daughters were born, my mother Lucy Estelle being the third in line.

Grandmother Bethel's mother was Georgia Ann Porterfield, born February 22, 1865, and died October 31, 1958. She was blind, and when we were very small, we would visit her in her bed. She would feel of her grandchildren and talk to us. I was a very small boy and was very impressed with her big house on the courthouse square in Danielsville, Georgia, in Madison Country. The Gordons and Rogers were professionals—doctors, lawyers, etc., as well we successful business operators.

Howard Gordon, Bethel's brother, was an outstanding Madison County prosecuting attorney. My dad would take me to see him try court cases. Back in my early life, lawyers would tread heavy on the Bible to prove their cases. One time, Great Uncle Howard did such a good job treading on the Bible that three jury members went down and got saved.

The Gordons were from Scotland. John George Gordon, in 1724, left Scotland and landed in Charleston, South Carolina, while still a young man. His wife was the daughter of Dr. Chapman, who did not approve of their marriage. This couple moved to Virginia and later moved to North Carolina. John George Gordon served in the Revolutionary army. My uncle Calvin Floyd did the research on the Gordon family. He married Georgia Rogers' mom, the second sister of the six Rogers girls. Uncle Calvin was raised on the other side of Rogers Mill River. As a very young boy, I visited them and their three children Felton, Harold and Eleanor. He became a postmaster in Atlanta and, for many years, he was the head postmaster at Conyers, Georgia.

My dad Ralph Vernon Bridges' family were of the Oglethorpe County, Georgia, origin. Dad was born April 4, 1915, at Lexington, Georgia, and died December 25, 1999. Dad is buried in Jackson County Memorial Cemetery in Commerce, Georgia. Also, my mom, Lucy Estelle Rogers Bridges, is buried beside him. You will find their plot close to the Bible statuette, as that is how my dad wanted her to be.

My three brothers and one sister will tell you no finer parents ever lived.

Even though I did not get to know my Grandpa Ben, my grandparents, Ben's parents, Wattie David Bridges, born March 28, 1881, in Oglethorpe County, Georgia, and died November 16, 1966, in Jackson County, Georgia, and Annie Leora Noell Bridges added much to my life. They are both buried in the T.O. Noell Cemetery in Oglethorpe County, Georgia.

If anyone wants to look at the Rogers-Bridges pedigree, I have in my files copies of both lines all the way back before and after they came to America. Take a look. You might be kin to us.

My Grandpa Bridges' dad was Richard Manoa Bridges. He was born March 7, 1848, in Oglethorpe County, Georgia. He died October 19, 1903. He married Lula Ellen Harris November 14, 1878. Richard Manoa was a farmer. He is buried in the Harris-Bridges Cemetery in Oglethorpe County, Georgia.

My Grandma Bridges' (Leora's) parents were Thomas Oscar Noell, born November 25, 1855, died April 20, 1934. He married Martha Jane Sanders, born August 29, 1860, died October 9, 1951. Both are buried in the T.O. Noell Cemetery.

My great, great, great grandfather was William Bridges. He was born before 1775 in Wake County, North Carolina, and died in November 1824 in Oglethorpe County. Georgia. His wife, Nancy Bridges, was born between 1770 and 1780 and died in May 1844 in Oglethorpe County, Georgia. William's dad was Solomon—known as James "the spy" Bridges, born 1755 in Virginia and died 1820 in Oglethorpe County, Georgia.

I remember living on Rogers Mill Road, on the end close to Highway 106. We could walk to Union Baptist Church. The time was the 1940s. We had no electricity or running water. We had a large garden for vegetables and had our own milk cows. I remember one Sunday, it was during WWII, and my dad Ralph had to work in the Bell Bomber plant in Toccoa, Georgia. He told my mom that our brown cow was missing and to tell our pastor at church to announce that the brown cow was missing and maybe someone might have seen her. We had a Mrs. Brown in Union Baptist, and she was out. The pastor announced that Mrs. Brown was out. My brother Ben thought he was talking about our brown cow. He jumped to his feet and said, "Dad said to tell you that she has one short tit." We broke up church that Sunday. Mom whooped him a little.

Our house on Rogers Mill Road in the 1940s was one with rock pillars holding it up. The front part of the house was close to the ground. The back of the house was built high, with lots of room and, as a small child, I could play under it. I remember that it had two bedrooms, one small, and a kitchen on one side with a hallway that separated a bedroom and meat-curing room on the other side. My brothers and I would sleep in that room, facing a large fireplace. Also, we had a fireplace in the large bedroom, which also served as a living room. We had no electricity, no running water, no screens on some windows. To this day, this house still looks the same on the outside. We had four water oaks out front by the road. I was riding my brother Thomas on my bike when he put his foot in the bike's front wheel. That threw us both into one of the oaks. It did hurt. We had fruit trees on all sides of the house. There was a very nice pear tree, which produced very large, nice eating pears. I remember our mom telling Thomas and me to leave the pears on the tree alone. However, we decided if we took one, she would not notice it missing. I helped Thomas climb up the tree to get a certain pear. Thomas fell from the tree, hurting his arm. That took some time to heal enough to be removed from a sling. Being the oldest that encouraged my younger brother to do wrong, she made sure my backside hurt for a while. But the talking my mom gave me really got to my conscience.

We had no power saws, so a crosscut handsaw was used to cut wood to cook with and to cut wood to heat our house. One day, Dad and Mom let me sit on a log they were cutting with the crosscut saw. They told me not to put my hand close to the saw. For some reason, I had the urge to see what the saw would do to my hand. Today I still have a large scar from my thumb to the middle of my right hand. I don't think we went to have a doctor fix my hand.

Do you remember the most scared you have ever been? I sure do! I was sleeping by myself in the small bedroom. I was around ten years old. The time was late August and there was a chill in the air. In the middle of the night, I awoke, raising up to reach toward the bottom of my bed to pull up a blanket. To my surprise, I felt a human arm that was very still. I thought, "If this is a person's arm, there must be a hand." Slowly going down the arm with my little hand, there was a hand, fingers extended. I tried hard to call Mom and Dad sleeping in the next room. Nothing would come. My voice was dead. That is the last thing I remember. The next morning, my bedroom window was pushed up. It had been closed. This room faced the road that ran by our house. Someone had come off the road, raised my bedroom window, then left my room after I passed out. If you have had a scarier time, I don't want to hear about it.

It seems that in my time after my birth, Mom would dress me up and take me to church and have pictures taken of her son. I have just finished writing my experiences breeding the short-horn breed of cattle for 50 years. I was first introduced to cattle around one year of age.

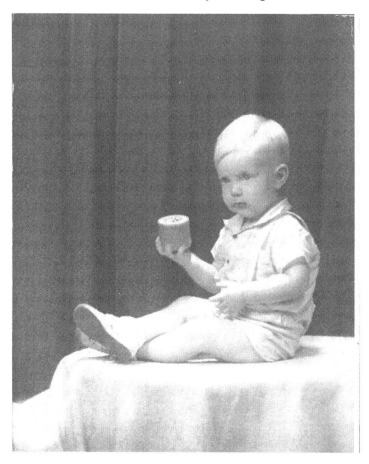

This picture was taken of me holding a box that, when you turned it back and forth, it would say MOO!

Along came my brother Ben Bridges on August 30, 1940. Then brother Thomas was born March 8, 1942, then on March 31, 1943, my brother Robert was born. Each time close to when my brothers were to be born, I would be taken to Grandpa's house or Grandma Rogers' for safekeeping. Grandma and Grandpa Bridges never owned any property, although they raised ten children. His family would move from farm to farm, where his children would help work a large farm along with any children the owner had. All during my childhood days, farming was hard, physical labor. My Grandpa Bridges was the farm manager overseer of the physical farm operation.

In 1943, when brother Thomas was to be born, Grandpa was living on a farm on the east side of Commerce. All children except his youngest, John, were gone. I was taken to their house. For some reason, I did not like their place, so I decided to leave. My grandparents had my Uncle John run me down on the narrow road that led to their house. They sat down to a hot bowl of powered tomato soup and it tasted so good. I had a desire to leave but changed my mind after soup. The time was World War II. Food was scarce. I remember my first-grade teacher, Mrs. Roxy Echols, telling us not to eat too much gravy because of the grease in it. This bothered me because, at the time, our cows were not giving much milk and Mom was adding more grease to the gravy we had all three meals. I remember my first-grade teacher, Mrs. Echols, was going around our classroom helping each student with reading. It seemed to me I was getting left out, so I jumped to my feet and hollered out, "I want to read." Patience is not one of my characteristics. Not long ago, my wife told me I had to do something because my teeth were getting yellow. I did something. I went out and bought me a yellow tie.

At the end of 1943, my dad Ralph was called in to go to the Navy, so he placed six-month-old brother Robert with my Uncle Lindsey's family. They owned a farm in the Moon Grove community of Madison County, Georgia. Dad located a place for us in Danielsville close to Grandma Rogers. This meant that I would now be in the second grade at Danielsville Grammar School. My teacher was Mrs. Baker. If a student got out of line, she disciplined with a wild onion across your arms. Try this. You will see that it really hurts. When wild onion switches were not available, Mrs. Baker would use a ruler across the palm of your hands. I remember one day that Grandma Bethel gave me a gallon of buttermilk to carry home, but I dropped it on the concrete sidewalk beside Hoyt Daniels Store. I cried the mile home, for I really like buttermilk and I knew that I had really let Grandma Rogers and my mother down. The high school and grammar school held a joint chapel program. The part I had was to get on stage and recite the poem "I Have Got the Fidgets." I also ran everywhere.

The war came to a close, and we moved back to our house on Highway 106 at the end of Rogers Mill Road. Brother Robert came back home, taking him a little while to learn that Uncle Lindsey was not his dad. It sure was good to be back to our farm away from city life in Danielsville.

It was not long before my brothers and I were back where we left off before the war. A small creek ran down the east side of the farm. It was joined by a larger creek on the very back. It was on the little creek that we would spend all our allowed free time, fishing and swimming. The large creek was a place where the creek ran straight into the bank and a large tree came from the back, forming a water hole where we learned to swim and catch our largest fish.

The Adams-Baxter farm was between our farm and Highway 106. One of my favorite ladies was Mrs. Callie Baxter. Mrs. Callie's husband was much older than her and unable to work.

Mrs. Baxter would work their land, plowing with two big grey iron-clad mules ("Iron Clad" referred to the steel shoes on their hooves). When I would go up to her house, she would sit me down to a large bowl of buttermilk cornbread, then save me a piece of the finest pie a person could eat. I got to know her granddaughter, Mrs. Jackie Archer, who worked out of our Nicholson, Georgia, post office. We would spend a lot of time talking about what was so great when we visited Mrs. Callie Baxter. Mrs. Callie's daughter, Annie May, and her husband, Buford Adams, lived just above our house. They had one daughter, Willa Anna, a little older than me. There were several other Adams also that lived in the Union Church-Rogers Mill community. When a new baby was born in our community, our mom would take me and my brothers to see the new baby.

One day, Mom said, "Mrs. Adams has a new baby boy so we need to go see him and brag about what a fine little boy he is. Now, there is a little something wrong with his ears, but if any of you boys say anything about them, I will knock you into next week." Looking at Mrs. Adams new baby boy, we said, "Look what fine muscles. And those beautiful eyes." Mrs. Adams said, "The doctor said he had

20/20 vision." I spoke up, saying, "Well, it's a good thing, for he will never be able to wear glasses." That day, I learned never to say a word when my mom bragged on a new baby. Even today, some people think I talk when I should be just listening. In my defense, I had to do a lot of talking when I was a teacher of agriculture for 40 years.

My third-grade teacher was Mrs. Miller, fourth grade was Mrs. Sorrells and Miss Edna Ruth Gunnells. Note: I developed a crush on her and went to her wedding. Mom and Dad took me. They knew I had a special feeling for her. In the fifth and sixth grade, my class was moved to the high school building. My fifth-grade teacher was Mrs. Juanita Jackson and my sixth-grade teacher was Mrs. Freeman, known as Bat Lady. Mrs. Freeman was a large lady who delivered blows with a paddle known as a bat. One day, she told us sixth-grade boys we needed a paddling. Since we were getting big, she would require us to bend over our desks. There were two or three boys that took her up, thinking they were so tough she couldn't hurt them. However, when she got through with them, lots of tears flowed. Earlier in this writing I mentioned that I had a hard time being still.

Well, Mrs. Freeman just thought I was wiggling too much in my desk, so she said I was needing to bend over for a paddling. I knew she would hurt my small 40-pound body, so I just fell to the floor, balling up tight. Mrs. Freeman just let me lay, knowing my getting up would come. Just as I got back to my seat, my dad, who checked on his boys at school, came by to check on me. That night, when I went to the barn to milk and do my chores, Dad came to the barn. He took off his belt, laid me over a barrel, and rolled me across the barn floor. I decided Mrs. Freeman was my best route to go if I needed punishment.

I can list a large number of my classmates at Ila, but there were some who stood out in my memory. Larry Hix spent his adult life in Rome, Georgia. The Hix family cemetery is located on Highway 96 near Midway Farm Store. I went to Larry's funeral at the family cemetery. Jerry Chandler rode my bus, driven by Mr. Amory Swindle. At our school breaks, I played with William Hitchcock. I see him at Commerce Wal-Mart occasionally. Donald Kesler. Manley Morgan. We played basketball on the outdoor courts. We were not allowed to play in the Ila gym. However, I was on the Commerce High School basketball team and Manley was on the Ila basketball team. I played guard and enjoyed stealing the ball from him. We beat them and that was a game. Ralph, my dad, came to see me play, as he had played for Ila. Mary Glynn Thomas, Nelda Ann Minish—she married Crawford Whitsel. They rode my bus. I have visited with her at Commerce Carwash. Mary Burton Langford as clerk of court, Madison County, Georgia. Mary Burton helped me with my birth certificate when I retired from teaching agriculture. Pearly Hanley, Ray Hanley. A member of the Jackson County Tax Assessors. Dennis Marlow, whose wife Greneva tells me Pearly Hanley is the only woman who can keep white carpet as white as when it was installed on the floor. It seems that Pearly married into the McGee family. That is also Greneva's family.

On the Ila playground, the school had outdoor toilets. They were just wood buildings like the ones we had at home. No water to flush, just wood seats for use. However, the outdoor toilet building was where I saw small boys smoking lots of cigarettes and cigars, and no one cared. My daddy had made it clear to me that was off limits. I thank my dad that I have never smoked anything or drank any alcoholic drinks of any kind. I think that is a plus for me as a high school teacher. Today, all kinds of addiction drugs are available that we were not exposed to, thank God. For sports, Ila Grammar School (white building) had, in addition to the dirt basketball courts, a baseball field (no lights). Boxing was very popular and our teachers would issue us a set of boxing gloves at break times. I listened to boxing on the battery radio with my dad. I remember boxing Jim Scarborough, Howard Minish, and some of the smaller boys my size. I, being fast, could get lots of punches in, then win. Howard Minish became an airplane pilot and opened a lawn mower business in Commerce.

One day, I brought my saw in for service. Howard called to the front counter to his son, "Here, son. I want you to meet the man who beat the socks off me with a pair of boxing gloves." My classmate Doris Thomason was much larger than me. He wanted me to put the gloves on and box him—I won. I was very hesitant to box Doris but decided I could stay out of his way. That was so! As Doris was slow and I could move in and land lots of punches, dodging his heavy blows. This made Doris mad that he could not hit with gloves on and he wanted to take the gloves off and come at me with his bare fists. The bell for class rang and I was one glad little boy. One member of my class I will never forget is Joe Fred McElreath. Joe Fred lived at the end of Rogers Mill Road on Highway 98.

Each year in all of the five Ila years and two Danielsville years, we would bus in all grammar schools to

Danielsville for a sports field day. My event was the sack race. I competed in this event all seven years and never lost. Being small and fast, I could put my feet in the corner of the sack and cross the finish line as if I was not in the sack. One field day, teachers were not watching as they were visiting with each other. Joe Fred was taking on all comers in bare fist fights. I saw him beat five different boys bad, till no other boy would fight him. That was over 60 years ago, and I have never forgotten how well he could fight. On my way to Danielsville some years ago, I stopped by the store he operated at the end of Highway 98, Rogers Mill Road. I did not get to see Joe Fred, but members of his family. I let them know what I had seen him do as a fighter.

Back at home on Rogers Mill Road, my three brothers and I would help Mother on Monday wash day. We would draw water from out of the dug well, filling a black wash pot, then build a fire under it, heating the water in which we boiled our most soiled clothes. There were two metal tubs with cold water that had rub boards and a third tub for rinsing before hanging out clothes on the clothesline for drying. I want you to know, four small boys who played in the dirt with our favorite little red racer on roads made with a hoe could get a set of clothes dirty. Every time we would visit Grandma Rogers in Danielsville, she would first take us to her wash room, scrub our elbows, removing what she called "the rusty rusty." She would always boost our egos by telling us she did not have to do her other grandchildren the way she washed us. All her other grandchildren lived in the city and most of them played with dolls.

My brothers and I also made and played with what we called slang shots. They were two pieces of rubber cut from a car tire tube, tied to a forked staff, with the other end tied to a piece of leather to hold a rock. One day, we were out along the road in front of our house, shooting our slang shots, when Mr. Adams came out from behind a brush on the road. My

brother Thomas did not mean to, but he accidentally hit Mr. Adams with a rock from his slang shot. Mr. Adams told Mother what happened, telling her she needed to teach us to be more careful with those slang shots. After he left, Mother wanted to know which one of us hit Mr. Adams. Thomas said he did, but it was an accident. He was just cleaning it when it went off. I told her I could not tell a lie. It was Thomas. By this time she had cut a sure-enough whooping switch. Thomas had got up under the house so far the cats couldn't get to him. All morning, Mother would occasionally stomp on the floor, "Come on out, Thomas, and get your whooping." Around lunch time, Grandpa Bridges stopped by and Mother sent him under the house to get Thomas. When Grandpa got to him, I heard Thomas say, "What is the matter, Grandpa? She after you, too?"

I mentioned earlier in this writing the large water hole on the large creek on the back side of the farm. Mother and Daddy always took us boys up to Union Baptist for Sunday School and preaching. They talked to us about what was right and what were the wrong things in life that we should not do. I know that when I was called to give my life to Christ (saved), when I was nine years old, I listened to Reverend Carter and I felt a strong feeling that I had never had before or that I have never felt since. My granddaughter Garnette and her husband R.J. Gravel gave me a devotional book by Sarah Young entitled *Jesus Calling: Enjoying Peace in His Presence*. I answered Jesus' call that day. I became a Christian! My daughter Shannon that I lost to cancer at 46 in 2016 once told me, "Dad, I am so glad I was raised by Christian parents. I was baptized in a concrete baptistry vat on the side of a large creek. I know for sure I will join my family in Heaven!"

My mom and dad would take us to church and to visit family members in a 29 Model A Ford or 30 Model A Ford car. The gas tank was mounted above the motor, in front of the car's windshield. Gasoline would be put into the tank at this location. With a small rubber hose, a person could siphon off the gasoline into a container set below. Thieves and others called this method "using a Georgia credit card."

I remember a time Dad had a straight eight-cylinder Dodge. The car was fast. While I was riding in the back seat, a patrolman stopped Dad for speeding. He asked me, did I want him to take my dad to jail. I replied, "Please don't." He gave Dad a warning. The big problem with the straight-eight Dodge was that it used a lot of gasoline. Dad sold it to a man. I remember him telling Mom and me that it had a one-half tank of gas and he was hoping that was enough gasoline to get the man out of sight.

For our crops, we grew corn from which we would pull the leaves from the stalks by hand. We called this farming technique pulling "farter." You would get as many leaves as your hands could hold, then tie them together with a leaf. Four hands tied together was called a bundle. Bundles were stored in the barn to feed our mule. We grew wheat that was cut with a wheat cradle. I have a wheat cradle in my possession now. There was a man in the Rogers Mill Community who would bring a combine by our house to thrash the wheat grains from the straw. With big families, we wanted watermelons to be large—100 pounds if possible. There was no such thing as a seedless melon. Now, we buy 20-30 pound seedless watermelons.

I remember we would store our sweet potatoes, which would keep outside all winter. The hickory poles were tied at the top like an Indian teepee. Then a door was fixed at the bottom. The sweet potatoes were placed inside the poles at ground level on a nice bed of dry pine needles, from bottom to top, inside the poles, which were a strong type cardboard, secured well. Then we built from top to bottom a layer of pine straw and placed insulation material over the pine straw. We covered it from top to bottom with a layer of red clay. We covered the tops of the poles with some type material that sheds water. We then would remove our crop of sweet potatoes from the fields, clearing off the dirt but not washing them. Then we placed them in this storage facility. Note: We had to remove the sweet potatoes from the field before frost or the potatoes would have a bitter taste.

I got introduced to rabbit hunting when I was 4-5 years old. When snow came, my dad would take me to show me how you could track a rabbit to his bed and have him for lunch.

All during my years, I learned to enjoy a good pack of dogs on the trail of game. Today I have my own special breed for trailing rabbits. I called them my rabbit masters and now, in my mature years, I take them out on my farm on Richard Bridges Road for pure enjoyment.

For some reason, when I finished sixth grade, my dad decided to move us to a farm between Danielsville and Comer, known as the Bond farm. This house had electricity. That could have been his reason for moving. It was good now not having to light lamps. We still had to farm with mules. Cotton. I remember when I was put to plowing at eight years of age. I was at my Uncle Lindsay Bridges. Grandpa Bridges was there. They both decided it was time for me to learn to plow. Being small, I could not hold to the plow handles, only to the bar between the handles. When they thought I had plowing under control, they left to get some cotton seed.

Back then, we heard of a lot of people talking about seeing signs telling them what to do. It was one of those hot July days, sun beating down. I looked and saw at the end of the field a person, who was waving and shouting, "Kenneth, stop the mule, throw down the lines, get out of the field." I got to looking and it was me. So I took it as a sign. I left the field, got on my knees making myself a promise not to ever plow with a mule again. Trouble was, Uncle Lindsay and Grandpa did not believe in signs. They ran me back in the field and I plowed crops with mules for several more years. Tripp Rogers, my cousin, calls me the last of the mule plowers. I remember the Bonds had a mule; the best I ever plowed with. The mule ran smooth and at a steady pace, always knowing what she should do.

When we moved to our new location, we took all the animals we owned. We had a one-mule wagon. I remember one day my dad hitched our mule to the wagon for me to go to the backside of our pasture to bring some firewood back to our woodpile at the house. I was standing in the back of the wagon and I started looking up at a buzzard overheard. I did not recognize that the buzzard was drifting back of me, and I fell off the wagon head first. I was not hurt, quickly jumping back on and taking the lines, continuing on for the wood.

We had lived at our new location for about six months when I found a narrow 3' ditch with 4' deep water about 100 yards long. There was a small spring, and someone had placed catfish in this hole of water. My Grandpa Bridges, who liked to fish, came by for a visit. I got him to go fishing with me, but when he saw where I wanted to fish, he said, "I'm going back to the house." However, he was not there long when I came to the house, showing him a large catfish.

Grandpa said, "Kemmy"—that is what he always called me—"You are the only one I know that can catch fish on dry land."

We were at the Bond farm for a little more than a year before we moved to a small farm on the east side of Commerce. While we were at the Bond Farm we helped build the plantation gas pipeline across it. The big dozers and tractors were a big attraction for me and my three brothers. We found some small steel ball bearings the size of marbles. I was going to school at Danielsville in seventh grade and as when I was in Ila school, we would play a game with small glass marbles. A circle was drawn in the dirt, the marbles would be placed in the center, and each person in the game would see how many they could knock from the circle by shooting another marble from the top of one's thumb. We would call that marble the Aggie marble. Why, I don't know. We could use the small steel marble as an Aggie to shoot at the glass marbles in the center of the ring. The steel Aggie was really effective. My seventh-grade classroom had a large coal-burning stove for heat. Our teacher's name was Mrs. Adams, and there were some overgrown boys that she had to paddle a lot. One day when she stepped out of the room, Richard Porterfield threw one of her paddles out the window. Richard had told me that I had to give him one of my steel Aggies or he would give me a bloody nose. The time was just past Christmas, and I had received a pair of Red Rider leather gloves. I placed my steel Aggies on the coal-burning stove, let them get hot, picked them up with my gloves, laying them on my desk. Along came Richard like he was going up to trim his pencil. On his way back to his desk, he scooped the two steel Aggies into his back pocket. After sitting down at his desk, he let out a yell, loud. He was hung up in his desk when our teacher Mrs. Adams came running with her paddle, "Shut up. What is the matter with you? You got fire ants in your pants?"

"No, ma'am. Hot steel balls." I might add you could keep other people's marbles if your mom didn't find it out. We attended the Danielsville churches and joined the Baptist. There we paid to have a stained glass window put up in honor of my mother Lucy's dad Benjamin Rogers.

When I moved to the East Commerce farm, I started my eighth-grade school year. We had moved there because my dad Ralph V. Bridges was working as a bundle boy in Commerce Blue Bell plant. A bundle boy was the person who brought cloth for sewing to the seamstress sewing pants or blue jeans together.

All during my childhood, I saw men treating cows for what they called Hollow Tail Hollow Horn disease. They would make a slit at the top of a cow's tail, pour in salt as a disinfector, wrap the slit up, put them in the barn, feeding them well and they would get better. Later in my life, taking animal nutrition courses, I learned they got better because it was not Hollow Horn Hollow Tail but hollow belly. Keeping them up and feeding them well really put back on the flesh they had lost.

Starting as an eighth-grade student at Commerce High School became an exciting year for me. I lived close to high school. My three brothers had to go across to the grammar school located close to Commerce First Baptist Church. This church is where my wife, Marilyn, and I attend church. I could walk to high school in five minutes, but I had to walk over to the grammar school for lunch. The house we moved to at Commerce had full electrical wiring. We could plug a radio into the wall circuits. All during my early years of life, we only had a radio that ran by battery. I remember that on Saturday night people would come over to our house. The "Grand Ole Opry" would be broadcasting the country music we liked. We would take off the station knob on the radio so no one could change stations. If the battery got weak you could heat it up at our open fireplace and it would recharge. My mother, during ironing and preparing our lunch, would listen at the soap operas "Stella Dallas" and "Ma Perkins." One day, my dad came through the house saying, "Why are you listening to their problems? We have enough problems of our own." My wife Marilyn's aunt Callie from North Carolina told us a woman at their prayer meeting asked for pray for a women on "At the World Turns." She was very concerned for that woman. Would you believe now in 2017 that there is a soap opera, "Downton Abby"?

While in the eighth grade at Commerce, we did not work cotton or other crops. After school I could walk over to the dirty basketball court and sharpen my basketball skills, working hard on developing a hook shot. Basketball was my sport, but football was the big sport at Commerce. I remember large crowds. At one football game, the referee marked off a 15-yard penalty against Commerce. A lady from the stands hollered, "Referee, you stink." The referee took the ball and stepped another 15 yards. He hollered back, "How do I smell from here?" Attending Commerce High School grades 8-12, we never had a gym for playing basketball. Nicholson High School had a gym, Ila had a gym, but not Commerce. I also enjoyed football, but I could not play because during football season I would be picking cotton by hand.

The biggest memory of eighth grade was that I failed algebra. Sitting behind me in algebra was this pretty little blonde girl with pretty brown eyes. There was no way I would pass this class. Mr. T.J. Jackson was my algebra teacher, and also my science teacher. I remember we were studying about the moon when Mr. Jackson told us the moon was 90,000 miles from the earth. I got his attention, asking how do we know that distance because no one has ever been there or could measure the distance. Mr. Jackson said, "Well I am your science teacher and that is what I expect you to put down when I put it on a test you are going to get." I did enjoy studying science and passed that class. Mrs. Edwards was our librarian. She demanded that everyone keep quiet and no loose motion. That "no loose motion" was my problem in Mrs. Edward's library, as I would wander around. One day, Mrs. Edwards said, "Kenneth, I see you have a spelling book. What is the name of it?"

I answered, "It says New Spelling Goal, but it's old." This answer really caused the older upper-class boys to break out laughing. They would, after then, tell me to say something else funny, but I started staying in my seat, started reading horse and dog books. And reading lots of books really paid off in my future college career.

Today, I gave my Rabbit Master Hounds some syrup from a plastic syringe. This helps keep the body sugar level up during this hot July weather. This reminded me of our eating sorghum molasses as a small boy. There is an art to all this. You take a plate with a flat place in the middle and a flange around the middle of the plate. Our mom would bake big cathead biscuits. You are to pour syrup in the middle of the plate, then add cow salve butter. The way you could tell if you had the right amount of butter, you take a cathead biscuit, drag it through the butter and if the biscuit broke in half you have the syrup and butter just right to eat. I remember one day we four boys were doing our mixing of butter and syrup when, all at once, Mom slapped Bennie back from the table. She told him, "How many times have I told you to lick that knife clean before you put it back in the butter?"

The big talk today and great excitement is that on August 21, 2017, we are going to have a total eclipse of the sun. Things are going to get dark and people are going to great expense to be at a ringside seat, such as at the North Georgia Mountains. Motels are sold out. The top of Brass Town Mountain, Georgia's highest point, seems to be the place to be.

This reminds me about an eclipse Grandpa Bridges told me about that occurred in 1918. He said that, after dinner that day, he had been back in the field plowing his mule in the cotton for about three hours when the sky just starting to get dark. Remember there was no warning, no way of knowing when an eclipse would occur back on those days. Grandpa said he unhitched the mule from the plow and after he got in the house, Grandma Bridges had supper ready, so they had the blessing, read some Scripture from the Bible, and went to bed. He remembered telling her, "Sure seemed like a mighty short day." They had only been in bed for a short while when it started getting daylight. Grandma Bridges said, "Walt, you thought that was such a short day, now what do you think of this night?"

Another big topic here in July and August 2017 is our major league baseball teams. After our Wednesday night prayer meeting Bible study, our pastor, who is a big fan of baseball, was discussing the Atlanta Braves. I told Rev. Carlton Allen that I had only been to one Braves baseball game. Some friends got me to go. We were sitting in the stands when a player named Dale Murphy hit a ball that came right up to where we were sitting. There were a lot of people trying to get the ball. I just held up one hand and the ball bounced up into it. Fans were just a-clapping me for my catch. I just stood up and threw the ball back onto the field. No one would talk to me after that. We always just had one baseball and if someone ran off with it they would be called a thief. I did play some baseball. We called our team the Berea Farm Team. There was a baseball field at the Wilson Junior Schoolhouse that we would play other pick-up teams in our area. There were no lights at this field, but the umpire would let you play until almost dark if the game was close to being over. We were playing a team out of Banks County and winning by one run and had two outs and two strikes on their batter. One more strike and we would win. I was playing catcher, and James Chandler was pitching and called a time out. It had gotten so dark you could hardly see. I went out to the pitcher, telling him it was time for our ghost pitch. I kept the ball in my mitt. James wound up turning loose a pitch. I slapped the mitt. The umpire called, "Strike three. You're out." The batter called out my foot. The ball was a foot over my head.

One problem we had was it was sometimes hard to get a volunteer to call the game. I remember a time we talked a person into umpiring when calling balls and strikes. He called a lot of pitches balls. The bases became loaded from the pitches that were called as balls. There was a batter up. He had called three balls. At the next pitch, he called, "Four. You are out." The batter asked, "Why am I out?" The umpire answered, "The bases are loaded. There is no place to put you. You are out!"

Chapter 2

Childhood Memories

Here in 2017 I have been hearing that there is still a lot of rabies, and each year I bring my Commerce vet doctor Kimsey Phillips to my Rabbit Master Kennel for their annual shots for their protection against rabies.

I am reminded that when I was about twelve years of age, living on Rogers Mill Road, rabies got me in trouble with Mom and Dad. Back in the late 1940s we referred to a dog that had rabies disease as a mad dog due to the behavior of the dog with the disease. As I remember, at that time there was no vaccine to prevent rabies. There had been reports that a mad dog had been seen in our area and Mom and Dad told us to be on the watch for the mad dog. We were coming up the hill on Rogers Mill Road that was just below our house. For some reason, I decided it was a good time, even though I didn't see the mad dog, to play a joke on my three brothers who were on the hill with me. I turned around, looking back. "Let's run. I see that mad dog coming." To my surprise, the youngest of us, Robert, took to running, crying hard. I knew it would not be good if he beat me to my parents in his condition because of my joke. I was at least four years older than Robert and running as hard as I could, but he beat me to Mom and Dad. Be careful how you joke. It could be, as I learned, that the joke was on me. To teach me the seriousness of my joke, I got a big-time whooping.

Now in 2017, my brother Robert lives in Statham, Georgia, where he has been mayor for about 17 years. Robert's hobby in life has been restoring old Ford cars and trucks. From a T Model truck to a 1965 Mustang Ford.

Robert has a large building full of restored Fords. I was impressed. He gave a copy of a handwritten letter that was sent April 13, 1934, to Henry Ford from the bank robber and outlaw Clyde Champion Barrow. I would like to quote this letter:

Mr. Henry Ford   April 13, 1934

Detroit, Michigan

Dear Sir:

While I have still got breath in my lungs, I will tell you what a dandy car you make. I have drove Fords exclusively when I could get away with one. For sustained speed and freedom from trouble, the Ford has got every other car skinned and even if my business has not been strictly legal, it don't hurt anything to tell you what a fine car you got in the V-8.

Yours truly,

Clyde Champion Barrow

We only lived in Commerce for one year and when school was out my parents moved the family to a 155-acre farm that we could rent for $100 a year. My dad's older brother Richard owned and lived on the adjoining farm.

Between our farms is located a very old cemetery, and as I watch the news in 2017, there is a lot of fighting and demonstrations going on in cities of the United States. There seems to be groups of people who want to remove all signs of our history of the Confederate soldiers who fought and died for their cause between the states. In this old cemetery, there are a lot of Confederate soldiers' graves.

History was one of my best subjects in high school. Mrs. Shepherd was a great American history teacher. The Civil War was not fought over slavery! Even George Washington had slaves, as well as many other people who lived north of the Mason-Dixon Line. Mr. Burel Taylor was also my government teacher as well as home room. The Civil War was, as most wars are, fought over economic issues. The North was industrial, the South largely agricultural. A large number of people who take part in today's demonstrations won't work for a living so they join riot crowds or any cause as a chance to destroy and steal. They need to take notice of what I found on a tombstone, get their lives together, go to work, contribute to society as true God-fearing Americans. I quote the tombstone they need to see and take to heart:

"Remember me as you walk by. As you are now, so once was I.

As I am now, so you shall be. Prepare for death and follow me."

When we moved, I was going into my ninth-grade year. I was to remain at Commerce High School and walk half a mile to Uncle Richard's house to catch Mr. Adams' bus in the morning. I would wait about an hour after school to catch a second load Mr. Adams drove after school. He would let me off on Hwy 334 and I would walk a mile home each afternoon. My three brothers, Bennie, Thomas, Robert, were to attend Benton School at Nicholson, Georgia. This school was close. To start with, they had to walk a half mile up to Uncle Richard's house because Benton was being in process of bringing in from Wilson Community School, located in the Berea Church area. After the consolidation was complete, a bus picked them up at our house. I wondered why I continued at Commerce High because Benton also had a high school, which was closed in 2016.

I was very glad I stayed at Commerce because starting with ninth grade, I chose to enroll in vocational agriculture class, FFA which, at the time, stood for Future Farmers of America. Mr. Roy Powell was my vocational agriculture teacher. He was a very large man who served in the U.S. Navy in World War II. Mr. Powell was also a veteran, an agriculture teacher teaching agriculture night classes to veterans of World War II. He also taught at Davis Academy before transferring to Commerce.

In our vocational agriculture class, we were to choose a crop or livestock project which would teach us important work and taking responsibility as well as gaining agricultural knowledge of growing food and fiber for our families. After I became a teacher of agriculture, I remember Oconee County High School when taking a class on a bus to see one of the student's swine projects. A student on the seat behind me was telling another student that he needed a swine project. The reply was, "No, no. That is too much work with responsibility." Could that be a problem in our country today, 2017? I think today many of our workers never learned when growing up how to work and take responsibility. Also, when we work for a company, etc., we need to learn who the boss is and follow his directions. I remember sitting with some teachers at lunch. Our superintendent had told us teachers when we left the rest room to always turn out the light to save power. One teacher said he had been doing a study on this subject and he had decided you could save more power by leaving the switch on.

"What do you think, Kenneth?" he asked me.

I asked him, "Did the superintendent tell you to do a study?"

"No," he said, "just to turn the switch off when you left the rest room."

"Then my advice to you is up with the zipper and down with the switch."

When my brothers and I were young, we would break off branches from tree limbs and would each act like we were sword fighting with them. Not long ago I noticed two boys who had broken off the branches from a fruit tree doing the same as we had done. I told them, "Let me tell you two something." I said, "If you had of left them on the tree, they would have produced some fine, sweet cherries you could have enjoyed eating."

They said that they didn't believe it. I said that it was so! "Well, okay," they said, "but last year it produced plums."

I chose as my ninth-grade vocational agriculture project a one-acre cattle winter rye grass crop. We only had one mule and to prepare my acre of winter grazing crop I had to break up the acre of land with a small one-mule soil-turning plow called a sod buster. This took several hours of work. I would then sow the seed by hand with seed in hand, slinging my arm allowing release from my hand. This took less time, but to get seed covered I then would again take my mule that I would hitch to what we called a drag harrow. It had spiked six-inch teeth. Yesterday I got a call from Mr. Greg Pittman, "our Jackson County farm agent." Mr. Pittman asked me, and I agreed, to go with him to our county park at Hurricane Shoals. At this park has been assembled many things from past county history. There, under a very large wooden shed area, are large numbers of pieces of farming equipment from middle eighteenth century to middle nineteenth century. It brought back to my mind the many hours of hard labor working in 90+ degree sun as my three brothers and I worked plowing and hoeing cotton.

At this point, let me describe this farm Uncle Richard and my dad Ralph Bridges moved Mom and us four boys to. The land on this farm had been abused. The people who now inherited this land didn't want to do hard-labor farming. They had all moved to Florida but could not sell the land because it was willed to them and their heirs. Having children, some very small, they could not sell it until all of them reached 21 years of age. The deal my uncle and dad agreed to when Dad moved us there was that his three older boys, then any of us using their tractors, would plant around 20 acres of cotton on our farm for us to work with our one mule, to plow, cultivate, and hoe by hand and pick the cotton by hand. In exchange, we would help him combine his grain crop and help him pick his cotton crop, which covered more acres.

The land my brothers and I worked had been plowed when it was too wet, which makes the red clay very hard. It also had may rocks. Gullies had been allowed to form and it was sloping land requiring terraces that were built around the slopes carrying rain water to the ends of the fields. This slowed down soil from where we plowed from erosion, but formed large gullies. This land also had so many undesirable grasses and weeds that were very hard to control in row crops.

The house we were to live in at this farm was built of logs covered with what was called "weather boarding." In a large room that had a fireplace was a short stairway to the attic, and when at this location, you could view the logs. This room was the one we used as a living room. There was another room that had a fireplace that my brothers and I used as our bedroom. Bennie and I slept in one bed, with Thomas and Robert sleeping in another one. There were no closets in which to hang clothes, so we hung wooden poles across two corners of the room on which to hang our clothes. The house had no way to heat except wood burning in the fireplaces. It also had no running water. We had to draw water from a dug well located at the back of the house. On the opposite side of the living room was a small bedroom where our mom and dad slept. This room opened into a small room we used as a kitchen. We had a cook stove with an oven and a fire box for heating the stove. We would take out our one-mule wagon to the pine woods, cut down pine trees with an ax, and using a cross cut hand saw, we would saw pine wood the length of the stove fire box, split the wood into small pieces that were allowed to dry for cooking our meals and laying in our beds. If it snowed, a small amount of snow would come down on our bed. Also, you could see chickens that roosted under the house through the cracks in the floor.

In talking with my brother about our cotton farming experiences on our farm on Richard Bridges Road, Dad gave my three brothers a bucket of cotton seed and told them to use the seed, and when they finished using up all the seed they could stop and go fishing. After planting for a couple of hours, they still had quite a lot of seed. I was plowing at this time. They asked me what they should do. I told them, "Dad said just plant all the seed." They went to the back side of the farm, took their hoe, made a long trench, put in all the seeds, covering them up, then took to our creek fishing. About two weeks later, Dad was walking in the area and came up on the area where the seed was planted. Hundreds of small cottonseed had come up in the trench. Severe disciple was in order for them, which Ralph Bridges gave. Be careful where and what kind of life seeds we sow. They just might come up to haunt us later in life.

Robert also had told me that he met his wife Barbara at Grandpa Bridges' in Danielsville, Georgia. Grandpa had a Model A Ford parked back of his house. Robert said he would climb up on the Model A. He sat between the two headlights. This started his love for the Model A. He has restored five of them from ground level up. They are stored in Statham, Georgia, at his old car museum.

Robert and his wife, Barbara, were camping on Clarke Hill Lake Reservoir. I called him and asked him how was the fishing. He informed me that I had broken him from fishing. When he was about twelve years of age, I would take my brothers, walk them six miles to a lily pad lake located on Oconee River. We would fish, getting leaches on us, catch maybe two or three speckled catfish, then we would walk the six miles back home. Robert told me that he made himself a promise that when he got grown, there were three things that he would not do: go fishing, live on a muddy road, and pick cotton. Uncle Richard tried to get Robert to help him pick cotton, but Robert told him that he had planted the cotton, now he could pick it.

My tenth-grade year at Commerce High School was a good one for me. That was the year I decided that, in life, I wanted to be a teacher of agriculture. Also, it was when I became very interested in the shorthorn breed of beef cattle. I really got a lot from the vocational agriculture classes that my agriculture teacher, Mr. Roy E. Powell, taught. I remember crying when, at Christmastime, Mr. Powel told us that after Christmas he would be taking a district vocational agriculture job teaching agricultural mechanics to adults. This announcement came at my twelfth grade, just before Christmas break, and after Christmas Mr. Gilbert Arial needed my help. I wanted to be an agriculture teacher, not to waste part of my senior year before going to college.

When I was starting my tenth-year vocational agriculture class, I chose to get, train, and show a steer in what was then called the Commerce Fat Cattle Show. Mr. Powell wanted me to show this shorthorn steer. The cost would be $300, a price my parents could not afford. I did purchase a $100 Angus steer who really had a high, wild disposition. I fed him in our log barn and he finally trusted me to halter and brush him. I have in my picture book a picture of me leading him behind the Commerce band down Main Street. I told the judge at our FFA chapter show that the steer would kick him if he came too close, but he learned this himself upon approaching the animal. A member of our chapter brought the shorthorn steer; a calm great calf that won the show.

Commerce, Georgia, in the early 1950s was a small town. They had just built the Andrew Jackson Hotel, which was two stories, but I had not been inside it. This is the hotel where Bill Anderson wrote the country music hit "City Lights." In my tenth-grade year, my vocational agriculture teacher told us we were going to Atlanta. This is when I first had a chance to go inside a hotel. The walls in the Biltmore Hotel on Ponce de Leon Avenue were trimmed in velvet like my grandma's Sunday hat. In the corner of what they called the lobby was a box-shaped small room with a door that opened smoothly. A man with a fancy suit stood inside at a control module. As we watched, an old woman strolled across the lobby and entered into the box. The door closed, and the box rose up through the ceiling. My agriculture teacher, with the rest of us teenagers, watched as presently the box lowered back down through the ceiling and a beautiful, young red-haired lady emerged and strolled through the lobby and out the front doors. I asked Mr. Powell what was this contraption, and he replied, "I don't know but I'm going to get my wife and let her go up and down a few times."

In my ninth and tenth grades at Commerce, Georgia, High School, our U.S. President decided that there should be a fitness test for high school students. We were to meet, be timed by coaches on the 100-yard dash and mile run. A ninth or tenth grade boy should be able to run sixty yards in eight seconds, a mile in 6:30 minutes. I ran the sixty yards in six seconds, and the mile in five minutes twenty-five second, which is the record at Commerce High School till this day. The school burned down shortly after I graduated.

My choice of high school sports was basketball. Starting back at Ila and Danielsville grammar schools, I played on outdoor dirt courts. This was also true at Commerce High. We had no gym so we practiced on dirt courts. Also, at home I would play basketball while living on Rogers Mill Road when I was in fourth grade. At Christmastime, my parents gave us a basketball. There was a place where we placed a five-gallon bucket on the solid wall of our barn, with the ball even with that small ball opening. I learned how to make my basketball shots count.

The Commerce Telephone Company was owned by Mr. W.L. New. He also owned a telephone company at Thomson, Georgia. The company was located where now the Windstream building is located in 2017. He erected a tall telephone tower on land just above our farm previously owned by Mr. Victor Richie. Mr. Richie has built two small lakes on this land. One of these lakes was located close to our oak woods. My three brothers and I would slip off our clothes and go swimming in the pond. We didn't have any bathing suits. We kept a close watch our for Mr. Richie. We would always get back to the woods, put on our clothes, and slip away before he could get to the far side of the pond dam. I heard a country song called "Streaking." When this song was on the music charts, a lady asked me what I thought of the new fad streaking. I told her that we called it running naked, but if our parents heard about their sons running naked that we would be streaked.

Now in 2017, there are what are called "travel" baseball, softball teams for boys and girls. Mr. New really liked basketball so he formed the Commerce Telephone Company Travel Team of eighth and ninth grade boys age group. Mr. New was told that he needed me on his travel basketball team so he asked my dad, who said I could be on the team. Mr. New's team was a big help to my coached high school basketball and college basketball career. Our coach was Mr. Hugh Ragcliff, a man who was at one time was a pitcher for the New York Yankees. He worked for Mr. New and even in his middle-aged years he was a great player at any sport.

The rules for playing basketball were far different back then than they are today. There was only a two-point shot, no matter from where the shot was made. There was no three-second penalty for standing in the lane under the goal. If you were a tall person and could stand under the goal, you sure had a big advantage over small players. At that age, 13 or 14 years old, I stood 5' 2" inches and weighed 140 pounds.

As a small player I had to play a good position and be quick in movement. I became good at stealing the ball. Also, I had in grammar school in Madison County eighth grade Commerce, practiced a hook shot over my head and with lots of practice, I learned to make the hook shot over a tall player guarding me. I also worked on making shots from long distance. Mr. New scheduled our teams to play Athens YMCA, Athens High junior team, Nicholson and Gainesville Mills. We won most of the games. At half time at Athens YMCA, some of their players came to me asking me how I was making those hooks and long-range shots. After one game, my coach, Mr. Ragcliff, told me, "You could have made anybody's team tonight." By tenth grade I was playing with the Commerce High School team, with Mr. Parks assistant football coach as coach. I remember one afternoon

Mr. New had a game for his team at New Holland Mills. Coach Parks had me scheduled to play a night game with Banks County. Mr. New told Coach Parks that I would be there for the Banks County game. I played two full games that day but was to spend the night at my Uncle Benny Adams' house in Commerce and go to school from there the next day. After getting in bed that night for much-needed sleep, a sharp pain developed in my right leg in the muscle below my knee. Never had I had a pain of this degree before. I hollered and Uncle Benny came to my bed. He explained I had a leg cramp from playing too much ball. He showed me how to get the cramp out.

My twelfth-grade high school basketball coach was Mr. Graham Hixon. Mr. Hixon was a well-respected top coach with a high reputation throughout Georgia. He got me a full scholarship at Piedmont College at Demorest, Georgia.

I have in my possession a book called *Past Tense*. This book was prepared by the Madison County 4-H Heritage Seekers and was published in November 1981. I consider this book a good recall for the time, years ago, when I grew up as a small boy. Four-H Club members interviewed a lot of the older people of Madison County. I knew a lot of the ones interviewed because I lived and played with them when a young boy growing up on Rogers Mill Road. I would, at this stage of my writing, include some of the contents of *Past Tense*.

On the front cover is a beautiful tombstone, erected for Jacob B. White and wife Susan Ella White. The Whites are also related to the Rogers family and several are buried at the cemetery at Rogers Mill.

Madison County was formed in 1812 from parts of Franklin, Jackson, Oglethorpe, and Elbert Counties. Before 1784, the county had been Wilkes County and Indian land. Madison County was named for James Madison, who served as President of the United States, 1809-1817. The county seat, Danielsville, was named for General Allen Daniel, a prominent man in the newly formed county.

At the old Madison County Courthouse is a statue of Crawford W. Long, M.D., who was the first to use ether as an anesthesia in surgery on March 30, 1842, at Jefferson, Jackson County, Georgia, U.S.A. He was born in Danielsville, Georgia, November 1, 1818, and died at Athens, June 16, 1878. He said, "My profession to me is a ministry from God."

In the book *Present Tense,* Rodney Chandler interviews and tells the story of Mrs. Mildred Strickland, known in the Union Church community as Lady Cure All. She lived about one and a half miles from our house on Rogers Mill Road. When I was about 4 or 5 years old, Mrs. Strickland at Union Church would love and spoil me. I really took a liking to her and knowing where she lived, I would slip off and go down the one and a half miles to visit her. Some time ago, my wife and I saw Mrs. Mildred. She told Marilyn how I would slip off from home and come to her house. My mother, Lucy, would come get me, give me a whooping, make me promise I would not slip off from her, but it would not be long before I would be back at her house.

Mrs. Mildred Strickland recalls finishing the dishes on Saturday nights, getting the flashlight, and walking hand-in-hand to a neighbors' house, who had a radio. They would all listen to the Grand Ole Opry, then she and Paul would make the long dark walk back home. The neighbors she was referring to were the people at our house. This gave me, Kenneth Bridges, a chance to get some more of her sweet love and petting.

One of the county communities mentioned in the book *Past Tense* is the Rogers Community. This community was named after Mr. W.T. Obadiah Rogers and, in his day, Rogers was a small town that had a general store, a doctor's office, a barber shop, and a blacksmith's shop. He would give anyone an acre of land that wanted to live there so that they could build up the membership of the church (Rogers Baptist was built in 1913). He also gave an acre of land to build a colored church. It was now known as Rogers Chapel.

My dad, Ralph, and my three brothers were introduced to Rogers Chapel about 2:00 p.m. one Sunday afternoon. I was around 9 years of age, thus I can remember the event very vividly. Over in the Rogers Chapel churchyard were some black men with guns, and on the road on a bank were more black men with guns, and they were shooting at each other. Just as we got behind the men on the road, my dad pushed on the A Model Ford brakes and it went dead. There we were in the gun battle line of fire. Dad told us to get down in the car floorboard. Brother Benny was in the front passenger seat and, being slow to listen to Dad's instructions, was shoved down by Dad, busting his lip.

I remember there were some colored ladies walking around in the churchyard calmly, as if everything was normal. I will never forget how scared all of us boys were. It seemed like forever before the black men on the bank of the road quit shooting, jumped in their cars, and left.

Obadiah Rogers was from a family of eleven, four boys and seven girls. My Grandpa, Benjamin, was Obadiah's brother. Grandpa Ben was known as a very smart businessman. For example, he went to the Bank of Danielsville, talked to a lady who pointed him to the bank's loan president. He told the loan president that he wanted to borrow some money. The banker asked him what he had for collateral. Grandpa Rogers told him he had a $10,000 war bond. The banker told him he would loan him any amount of money on the bond, up to $10,000. Grandpa Ben told him he wanted to borrow a dollar for a year. What the banker said was, "We don't loan just a dollar!" Grandpa said, "You lied to me, then. You said you would loan me any amount on the bond, up to $10,000." The banker said, "You are right. I did tell you that, so here is your dollar. I will take the bond."

A year later, Grandpa Ben went to the bank, paid the note off for $1.25 with interest. As he was leaving the bank, the banker said, "It would sure be interesting to me to know why you just borrowed one dollar." Grandpa Rogers told him he needed a safe place to keep the $10,000 bond for a year. He said, "I talked to the ladies and they told me a safe deposit box would be $15. But you kept it for me for 25 cents."

I mentioned earlier in my writing that if you live in Madison or Jackson Counties you might be kin to the Rogers or the Bridges. In the first part of the 1900s, there were many families with 10 or more children. Now in 2017, I only know of two families with 10 or more children. In *Past Tense*, there are several families listed with 10 or more children in the family. The Jackson Hix family had 10 children. In his dad's family were 12 children. I played with Larry Hix, who had to have been some of the offspring of the Hix family at Ila Grammar School. The Hix farm cemetery, located on Hwy. 98, close to Midway Farm Supply and on this farm after I retired from teaching agriculture, cut hay for Mr. Jerry Paul Pittman. In the Willie Mae Evans Adams family, there were nine girls and two boys. Mr. B.H. Seagraves was born in Madison County in 1907. He was one of 16 children. His wife was one of 10 children. Let me mention Johnny and Ellie McElroy that had 11 children. In the 11 were two sets of twins. Two very good friends that are in my and my wife Marilyn's Sunday School class are Ricky and Vickie McElroy. Ricky tells me he had an uncle named Johnny McElroy. Ricky and Vickie live in the Rogers Church community. Ricky has several members of his family buried in the Rogers Church Cemetery. Now in 2017, probably one of my former vocational agriculture students I taught who has become very very rich is Zack McElroy who, along with another student I taught, Tony Townley, started Zaxby's Chicken restaurants. I am told that those two have around 500 chicken franchises throughout the United States. When I would visit my Uncle Lindsey and Aunt Isabelle Bridges, who lived in the Moons Grove Church community, they would often mention their good friends and neighbors the McElroys.

Ricky McElroy has lived in the Rogers community almost all his life. I talked about large families, and Ricky and I knew the Luke Perry family. There were 14 in their family. When I was 5-7 years old, I would visit them and eat at their large table. Ricky told me that Luke Perry would always take the family each year to the Athens Fair. One year, they had in a tent a prize bull they were charging admission to see. Mr. Perry asked the bull attendant how much would it cost to see the bull for his 14 children. The attendant asked, "Are they all of those 14 kids yours? Then we need to take the bull out and put you in and charge admission to see you."

Ricky told me that the Rogers community had a barber, Mr. Roy Adams. He charged 50 cents for a haircut. A lady wanted Mr. Roy to cut her hair. He asked her, "How much do you want me to take off?" She replied, "About 10 cents worth."

I mentioned it was a scary time at Rogers Chapel Church for us Bridges boys. It took a while for Benny's lip to heal after our car went dead behind the black men shooting at each other at Rogers Chapel. At this point, let me bring you up to date on Benny Bridges, the one who was my bedfellow for all of my childhood. In the Northeast Georgia News, the Anderson Independent newspaper, Friday, November 12, 1976, I would like to put in part of a story about Benny being picked the top peace officer for Georgia in 1978. "It's Been a Scary Year for Top Peace Officer":

"When he was a boy down on the farm, Benny Bridges decided he wanted more out of life than plowing a mule and picking cotton. He traded his cotton sack for a uniform and his mule for a Georgia State Trooper car."

The article states that:

"On a cool windy Saturday morning in June, Bridges' patrol car was flagged down by a woman on Thompson's

Bridge. The officer was told that a woman had just jumped from the bridge into the lake below. 'As I reached the bank, the woman surfaced. A man who was standing near the water line, which was 30 feet below the bank, told me that he couldn't swim, but if I could get her out, he would help me get her up the bank,' Bridges said. 'It was in June. The temperature was 58 degrees. Wind was blowing and when I dived into the water, I could hardly get my breath. I swam to the woman, got behind her, and pulled her out.' He later learned that she didn't want to live because her husband had died a few months earlier.

"A little later, Benny Bridges had an even more frightening experience. Benny said, 'I wasn't afraid during the lake rescue, but frankly, I was scared to death this time.'

"This time, Bridges spent an hour in a 1000-foot long, narrow, dark mine shaft in Lumpkin County, rescuing a college coed who had tumbled 160 feet down the vertical column of an old goldmine.

"Benny arrived on the scene around 10:00 p.m. and decided to go part way down the 1000-foot two-by-four foot mine shaft 'to size up the situation.' When he got about halfway down, he could hear screaming and knew he had to go on. He said he had never been in a mine before and he didn't know what might happen down there. He kept thinking about cave-ins and gas. Benny said, 'When I reached the bottom, I came into a 20-by-20 room. I could hear her from a shaft on the far side of the room. Half of the room was flooded, but the only way to get across to the shaft was to walk a foot log for about eight feet across open space.' After he crossed the foot log, reaching the girl, he found she had back, head, and leg injuries.

"Benny's problem was how to get her back across the foot log. 'She wanted to cross the log, and I wanted to get out bad, so we decided to try,' he said.

Benny got behind the woman and held onto her belt to give her balance. After crossing the log, he pushed the woman up the 1000-foot shaft. A man later told Benny that there was a 400-foot drop below that footing. He said he didn't know that. It just looked dark down there."

My brother was selected to be Peace Officer of the Year by 10,000 members of the Georgia Peace Officers Association. Benny went on to be Lt. Governor Zell Miller's main trooper for his time in office. He retired as captain of North East Georgia's State Patrol. He represented Habersham and White Counties for around 12 years in the Georgia State House of Representatives.

As the captain, he wrote lots of safety articles for newspapers and talked on radio programs. He told me that on one talk radio program, a man that both of us knew called in and asked, "Where is a person most likely to get killed in a car wreck?" He told him, "Within 12 miles of where he lived." He told me the man quickly moved!

Benny also told me one of his patrolmen stopped our dad, Ralph Bridges, asking him, "Mr. Bridges, do you know why I stopped you?" Dad, who always drove, even on a main highway, at 35 miles per hour, answered, "Yes. Because you cannot catch any of the others."

Our mother Lucy's sister, Grace Fowler, was riding with our Uncle Comer when one of his troopers stopped them. He asked Uncle Comer, "Do you know why I stopped you?" Uncle Comer answered, "No." The trooper told him, "You have a tail light out." Uncle Comer asked, "Which one is it?" Aunt Grace spoke up, "Now, Comer, I told you to get that tail light fixed two weeks ago."

Aunt Grace wanted to be a missionary when she was growing up, but her church could not finance her for foreign mission work, so she became a self-missionary, going later in life preaching at different churches. She always wanted her church offering to go for missions.

All during our childhood, we never had any plumbing in our home. All we had was an outdoor toilet called an outhouse. Many people have told me that, after he became a state representative, Benny went from the outhouse to the State House.

Growing up on our cotton farm, we did have some forms of recreation, mainly fishing. Hunting was my brothers' and my thing. I met with my brothers this past Saturday, September 23, 2017, at Cracker Barrel in Commerce. We talked about the hurricane that came across North Georgia early the week before. Never in all my years of living had I known a hurricane to leave the ocean, come all across North Georgia with high 50-60 miles-per-hour winds, raining steady for several hours, causing lots of damage. But now I can say I made it through one. But I hope one never comes my way again. We talked about when we were possum hunting at night with our red bloodhound, Old Red. People would eat lots of possum back in the 1950s. You would tree them and shake them out of the tree. They would hit the ground and play dead. You would put them in an enclosure, feed them sweet potatoes and other clean food to fatten them up and sell them. A small railroad ran not far from our house. My three brothers, Benny, Thomas, Robert, and I had our lanterns and flashlights, hunting close to this railroad when there came a train. My brother Benny started with his lantern, waving it and flagging down the train, which he stopped. The train conductor hollered, "What kind of emergency do we have here?" Benny told him he wanted to see if he would like to buy a possum. The train conductor told Benny that he must be an idiot, but his wife and he did like possum, and now that he had the train stopped, how much did he want for him? Benny really made the train conductor mad. He told him that we had not caught a possum yet, that he just wanted to see if he wanted one.

On another possum hunt, we were in Mr. Joe Garrett's pasture, which I knew there was a bad, mean Jersey bull. I did not hear the bull, but I made out like I did. I told my brothers, "We had better get up a tree," and I started climbing one. Benny and Thomas climbed up the tree right behind me, but when I looked for brother Robert I saw he was too scared to climb. He was on the ground, arms around the tree. In our adult lives, Benny and Thomas had good quail dogs. Today, I have a breed of rabbit dog on my cattle farm. However, I never have known Robert to do any fishing or any kind of hunting since our possum hunting days.

Back in 1954, the Georgia Power Company built a transmission line across the backside of our farm. When they came to the creek, they just dammed it up, crossing the small dam with their equipment. This made a great place for we four boys to go catfish fishing at night, but not with our parents' blessing being we were of such a young age. One night, we were at the creek and I had just caught a nice catfish when, across the creek up in the woods above us, a loud scream let out like someone had a woman by the throat. My brothers, sounding very scared, wanted to know, "What was that?" I, being the big brother, said, "Nothing. Just keep fishing." But it was a very short time sounding a lot closer to a scream sound again. I want you to know that we left that creek, leaving all fishing poles behind. Mom and Dad told us that a lady had been murdered in those woods some time back, and at certain times you could still hear her scream. That ended our fishing on Hardman Creek at night.

Beginning in the late 1980s, an effort was made to hold a Rogers Family Reunion, starting with the children of Mary and Thomas Rogers, as follows (11 children total):

1. Obadiah W.T.—married Tallulah Rice
2. Mattie—married Willie Williams
3. Lucy—never married, died at age 28 of lockjaw
4. Nannie—married Joe Webb, no children
5. Lloyd—married Cora Murray
6. Benjamin—married Bethel Gordon
7. Mitchell—married Minnie Tolbert, no children
8. Annie—married George Burroughs
9. Stella—married Eugene F. Hardman
10. Mary—married Charlie Pat Graham
11. Merle—married Bob Davidson

The Rogers Family Directory, a copy of which I have in my possession, was printed May 1991. The directory was put together by Mrs. Sandra Wardlaw, wife of Maurice

Wardlaw. It contains the names of children of all the above families and their addresses at that time. Sandra did an outstanding job, giving a lot of effort and time. Thanks, Sandra.

Several Rogers Family Reunions were held at Rogers Baptist Church, and I am including in this writing the reminder to the Benjamin Rogers family, of which I am a proud member. This was sent by Kathryn (Flowers) Edward for the grandchildren of Benjamin Rogers:

The grandchildren of Benjamin F and Bethel (Gordon) Rogers invite you to join them Saturday, September 19, 2009, to enjoy a get-together and a covered dish lunch at:

Rogers Baptist Church

1890 Rogers Church Road

Commerce, Georgia 30530

We will begin meeting at 11:00 a.m. and have lunch around 12:30 p.m. Bring a dish and plan your schedule so that you can stay for a time after lunch. We would like to have time to get better acquainted and share some remembered times of parents, grandparents, aunts, uncles, cousins, and family friends.

For about 10 years, we held this Rogers Family Reunion and had good attendance from all of the families of Mary and Thomas Rogers. However, now all of the older members have passed away. The younger generation had rather keep in touch by texting on smart phones.

Our Bridges Family Reunion that has been going on for many years was held on October 16, 2017, at Berea Community Center, with a great crowd attending. Our oldest member, who had just turned 95 years and was in attendance, was Mrs. Daisy Bridges Adams.

Chapter 3

College Days

I enjoyed my days at Abraham Baldwin Agricultural College, but it did not give me much time to date any of those pretty South Georgia college ladies. One of my benefits of going to college at Tifton was that I really got to know South Georgia. I was given the chance to visit different parts by going home on weekends with many male college friends. I would get to school in my second year at ABAC, 1956-57, with the 1952 mainline Ford car Dad and Mom provided me. I would occasionally bring a South Georgia college friend home with me. One friend I brought was a basketball friend named Phillip Simpson. Phillip Simpson was the key player on my ABAC basketball team. He went on to play for the Georgia basketball team where he was one of Georgia's top players. For entertainment, my brothers and I took Phillip for a possum hunt on Sandy Creek. We tracked a possum with our little redbone hound. It was up a hollow tree, with vines growing up over the top. Now get this picture: Little Red used the vines to climb up the dead tree to a hole at the very top. All of us were standing at the base of the tree when my brother Thomas decided he would climb up the tree to a little hole in the tree, just below where Little Red was looking down into the tree at the possum. All hell broke loose when, all at once, the little possum appeared at the little hole looking brother Thomas eyeball to eyeball. Thomas started backing down the tree and the little possum started down, still looking Thomas eyeball to eyeball. To us college boys on the ground, looking up, this was an extremely funny event. Thomas started backing as fast as he could, and the little possum kept coming. It seemed the only way Thomas would escape the little possum was to bail out of the tree backward, which he did. By this time, Phillip, our brother Robert, and I were laughing so hard we could not stand up. After picking Thomas up off the ground from the mud hole where he had landed, we all agreed that event was enough fun for one night, so we went home.

I have already mentioned some of the many things very worthwhile my brothers Robert and Benny accomplished in their adult lives. Now I want to mention the fact that my brother Thomas has made an outstanding accomplishment in his life also.

Thomas became a very good basketball player, earning a scholarship to play for Truitt-McConnell College. He earned his bachelor's degree in physical education at Berry College at Rome. He became a basketball coach at Commerce High School, where he took teams to the Georgia state finals. He completed his master's degree in education administration. He taught driver's training at Commerce High School. He was hired as principal of Maysville Elementary. Thomas and his wife, the former Miss Kathy Highfield, bought a farm in the Bolds Springs community of Franklin County. Kathy took care of boiler chicken houses and Thomas served as principal of Cartersville Elementary School. He became superintendent of Franklin County Schools. Thomas is now serving his second term as Chairman of the Board of Commissioners for Franklin County. All my brothers have outstanding families, and they also are contributing greatly to their communities.

Let me mention a different kind of fishing my brothers and I did in late summer. This type of fishing, to us, was called grapping. To some folks, it was known as noodling. The way we worked noodling fishing, we would take an old 1940 International pickup truck that our dad had bought from Uncle Comer Fowler. We would go to a lake on the Grove River close to Five Points between Commerce and Carterville. This lake would fill up when heavy rains came, and riverbanks would overflow, depositing fish into lakes. Each year in August, the old lake would dry down where you could take a sack, feel under the logs laying down in the water where you would find catfish laying still, grab them, and deposit them in your cracker sack. One time, I was feeling under a log and I felt something cold and rough—a snake. Denny Archer was on the opposite side of this log. I slowly withdrew my hand and, all at once, this snake came crawling down the log between Denny and me. I told Denny to stay calm and to remember this snake was just as scared of us as we were of him. Denny said, "If that is so, Kenneth, then this water is not fit to drink!"

To pay for my tuition at ABAC, I was given a job in the college dining hall. My responsibility was to open the college dining hall at 5:00 a.m., cook eggs, grits, pancakes for students' breakfast (8:00 a.m. three hours), go to class till 11:00 a.m., then wash pots and pans from large sinks till 1:00 (2 hours). Note: I cleaned all the pots and pans used to cook lunch for students with no help (2 hours) then from 1:00 p.m. to 4:00 p.m., back to class. From 4:00 to 4:30 p.m., haul food scraps to swine, ½ hour; from 5:00 to 7:00 carry food to girls serving students' supper (2 hours). My pay was 45 cents an hour. However, back then, tuition for a quarter (3 months) was $275.00. I paid all my tuition at ABAC, practiced basketball during the season 7:00-9:00, studied class lessons 9:00-11:00 p.m. Note: I worked the above schedule for two years. My dining hall dietician and food instructor was Mrs. Margarite Vanderhoef. She worked in my Tabac school 1956 annual. Best wishes for the future, remember the success for your future will be great if you keep up the kind of effort you have given the ABAC dining hall.

At ABAC, my room was in Weltner Hall. My dorm mom house director was Mrs. W.M McGhee. I really liked her the two years at ABAC. She treated us like sons. I have noticed the moms take care of their sons. Let me tell you how much she cared for the boys under her watch. One night, someone threw the main electric circuit breaker, throwing all the campus into darkness and hollered, "Panty raid." Mrs. McGhee was standing outside our dorm, hollering, "It is not any of my boys!" I knew better than to even give that raid a thought, but standing close to Mrs. McGhee, I saw lots go and come back to Weltner Hall. Mrs. McGhee always considered her boys the best ones on campus.

I mentioned early on in my writings that I started developing my basketball skills by shooting at a 5-gallon bucket nailed to the back of our barn when I was 6-10 years old, living on Rogers Mill Road in Madison County. All through grammar and high school, I worked on these skills and played with the ABAC team.

I am sitting now in my front yard under the big oak at my house on Richard Bridges Road, October 20, 2017, looking up at my 1956-57 ABAC yearbook. Reading what people, fellow students, wrote about me brings back lots of good memories. However, I know it's always good to review what was a very important time in a person's life. My roommate was William Doke from Midville, Georgia. We wrote about what he would never forget: a one-on-two basketball game we played.

Even when it was not basketball season, a member of the team would be provided a basketball for practice in his or her spare time. I was shooting baskets by myself at the gym when Will and a friend of ours we called Alabama showed up. Alabama was 6'8" tall, William around 6' tall, and me being about 5'5" at that time. These two came out to challenge me to some basketball games up to a score of 21 points. I accepted their challenge. The first game ended with Kenneth scoring 21, them 2 points. I think they thought being much taller, Alabama would stand under the goal, William would throw him the ball which I could not reach, and he would score. The game started at half court and most of the time I stole the ball from William or knocked it away from Alabama if he ever got the ball, after three games of each being the same results. For some reason, Alabama got mad and wanted to fight me. I told him to take off his glasses. Eyesight was one of his problems. After he laid his glasses on a bench at the side of the gym, he started my way, fists ready for a big fight. I thought I could hit him with an overhand right, but for some reason I threw a left-hand punch, which landed right between his eyes and nose, causing his nose to start pouring blood. Alabama went straight to a bench, holding his nose. That ended the fight. After about two days, Alabama's eye was, as well as his nose, blue black. William and I had not told anyone what had happened. The boys on campus started asking him, "What happened to you?" Alabama's answer was that he had run into a door knob. They said, "How did you run into a door knob? Were you down on your knees crawling in and out of your room?"

After my two years of ABAC, I returned home, transferring to UGA at Athens, Georgia. I would be commuting in a 1951 Ford coup my parents would furnish me. Both my mom, Lucy, and dad, Ralph, were working at Carwood Manufacturing Company at Winder, Georgia. This company made shirts and work pants. They got me a job at the plant, moving the finished shirts and pants to locations for shipment. This meant that I would be moving throughout the plant, to outside the building, where they were shipped. Each day at midmorning, we were allowed a 30-minute break where we could cross the street in front of the plant to go to a store for refreshments. At this store, I met a young girl by the name of Mary Ellen Davis.

Mary Ellen told me that she had just finished the 11th grade at Buford High and that she lived on Flowery Branch Road that was up 124 about 7 miles north of Braselton, Georgia. For some reason, from the first time I met Mary Ellen, I knew I wanted to make her a big part of my life, so that was what I set out to do.

Chapter 4

Early Teaching Memories

When working that summer at Carwood Manufacturing, I rode to work with Mom and Dad. I was not
needed at home with my brothers, who were now old enough
to manage on their own. All of them were well along in high
school, with my brother Benny able to drive. We had sealed
down our cotton crop acres, but Uncle Richard was still
going strong with cotton. However, he had lost his two oldest
sons to the Army. The Korean War was in process. Julian
was drafted into service and Willard had taken a job in the
Commerce Cotton Mill. They were getting into the chicken
business, growing broilers.

All during my work at Carwood, I was making sure I
learned everything possible about Mary Ellen Davis. I
learned that when she was about 2 years old where she was
born in Miami, Florida, her mom and dad had separated. Her
dad stayed on in Miami, but she and her mom moved back
close to her mom's brothers at Buford, Georgia. Her mom,
not long after, married again. In the next 13 years of her life,
three half-brothers were born into her family. They were very
poor. In fact, they lived in an old Barrow County
schoolhouse with her stepdad and her brothers cutting
pulpwood for a living. Mary Ellen, at 13 years of age, was
asked to come live with her Uncle Marion and his wife to
help with their only child, now late teens, who had a muscle
disease.

After our summer of working at Carwood, I started
my commute to UGA, working on my degree in Agricultural
Education, and Mary Ellen entered her senior year of high

school. We started dating once a week, beginning with going to the church she was attending, Mt. Moriah Baptist, and also Sharon Baptist, close to Braselton. We had no way of calling each other, for neither house had a phone. Therefore, I made sure I sent Mary Ellen a letter each week, to let her know I deeply cared for her, and we had to work out which weekend night that I might see her. To my later surprise, I learned that she kept neatly in a small box all the letters I wrote her for two years. I now have these letters for 1957, 1958, and part of 1959 in my possession as I am writing this in October 2017.

Mary Ellen Davis was a very smart, as well as beautiful, young woman. She was one of the very top of her high school graduation Buford High School class. All during my junior third year of college, she could help me with my agricultural studies. I was taking an entomology class (science of study of insects). She was not afraid of bugs, so she helped to gather them for me to classify the 100 different insect families as a class assignment requirement.

But when she graduated, Uncle Marion Davis did not believe that women needed much education. Mary Ellen got a job at Sears & Roebuck on Ponce de Leon Avenue in Atlanta. She rode with some local people to work 40 miles each way. She was one of the best in shorthand, working all kinds of secretarial work. She worked the big adding machines in the Sears Accounting Department.

In January 1959, I could not be apart from the love of my life, Mary Ellen, if she was willing to accept my proposal to be my wife. It definitely was one of the happiest days of my life when Mary Ellen told me she would be my wife. We planned our marriage for after completion of my junior year at UGA, which ended in March. On March 27, 1958, Mary Ellen Davis became Mrs. Kenneth R. Bridges.

Mary Ellen had gotten me a job also at Sears where she worked. I packed window shades for work. We rented an apartment close to our work. That was the place of our honeymoon. Our landlady lived on the other side of the old house, which had a long hallway between our side and her side. Our rent was $40 a month. However, she kept a close watch on me and Mary Ellen, and she just happened to be in the hallway close to our side door a lot. She could start a conversation and would talk so fast she would forget the subject and want to know what we were talking about.

Mary Ellen's furniture was still at Uncle Marion's and Aunt Mary's house, and they invited us to move back in with them, which after the end of our one month of rent, we did.

For the rest of the spring and summer we drove to Sears to work. Beginning the fall quarter of UGA I went back to complete my agricultural education degree. I would take my wife to the bus station at Lawrenceville to catch the Greyhound Bus to Sears for her work. I would then go to Athens for a day of classes. After classes were over, I would drive back to Lawrenceville, pick Mary Ellen (my wife) up, and go back to our house. This we did for the rest of the year 1959.

Starting the winter quarter of 1960, I was ready to go out for my three months' apprentice teaching. I was assigned to go to Lavonia, Georgia, to teach under the supervision of Mr. Loy Smith, teacher of agriculture at Lavonia High

School. Assigned to Lavonia also was Terrill Benton who graduated from Jefferson High School. Terrill had been a national FFA officer. Terrill Benton was also married to the daughter of Judge Mark Dunahoo. Judge Dunahoo was to play a part in the murder trial of Cliff Parks for the murder of Floyd Hoard. We roomed at the Davis boarding house there on the square of Lavonia near the high school. I was assigned to teach one ninth-grade agriculture class and the Fairview Community of Franklin County for my requirement of teaching agriculture adult classes. Terrill was assigned to Lion community for his night adult class work.

I enjoyed teaching my ninth-grade students. After school I would visit different students' home projects. Also, after school we would work toward getting to know the people who lived in our night adult class community. I taught a night adult class on farm rat control. This was just when Warfarin for rat control came on the market. Now in 2017, they give it to humans for a blood thinner. There were community club houses with propane gas heat, for the heater inside the building there is a turn-off valve. There is also a turn-off valve outside the building at the big propane gas tank. Both valves should be turned off when the building is not in use. However, one night when I turned the outside valve on and went inside to light the heater, someone had not turned the inside heater off. Some gas had leaked inside the building and I got a surprise when the heater lit! I did not get burned, but I sure got a good scare.

I remember it was sheriff election time in Jackson County with John B. Brooks as sheriff at that time on the ballot. I went home to vote against him. Terrill went home to vote for him. He told me he would let their farm workers out of jail quickly if they got drunk and were locked up. The sheriff always went and picked up ballot boxes at closing time, delivering them to the courthouse for tally. In the late sixties, when Brooks was convicted of allowing car theft and bootlegging in Jackson County, it was reported that he would send two men to graveyards to write down names of voting. One time, one man told the other man that had taken him that they must take down names also from the other side because they had just as much right to vote as the ones already written down. Jackson County in the fifties and sixties was known as the center of what was called the Dixie Mafia. Of the 159 counties in Georgia today, it is still the only county the GBI does not have to contact to hold investigations in Georgia without the consent of the sheriff.

After the three months of practice teaching, I was to complete my Bachelor of Science Degree, one quarter left— April, May, June. My wife, Mary Ellen, was still working at Sears, so we used the same transportation as before apprentice teaching so I could finish work on my degree. However, of all the many science courses I passed, there was one physics course I still did not have credit for (a 5-hour physics 60 course). I had taken it once at ABAC and once at UGA, and the different teachers stressed different physics math interactions of science. My wife made me study and she studied with me and I passed the course and got my degree. Now ready to start the agricultural career I had wanted since tenth grade at Commerce High School. Now to get a job!

My Northeast Georgia district supervisor was Mr. J.H. Mitchel. Mr. Mitchel's responsibility was to place new teachers of agriculture where openings for teachers of agriculture occurred. Teaching vocational agriculture is a 12-

month job. The year starts July 1 and ends June 30 of the following year. My high school vocational agriculture teacher was Mr. Roy Powell who, at this time, was working out of Mr. Mitchel's office. Conner Hall UGA had highly recommended me. Mr. Mitchel contacted me the last week in June 1960, telling me he was ready to put me to work teaching vocational agriculture. He told me he had two openings for vocational agriculture teachers, one in Blairsville, Georgia, and the other opening at Crawfordville, Georgia. He told me he was placing me at Blairsville, Union County. Taking me to Blairsville, he had the superintendent of schools, Mr. Pat Helton, sign a contract with me. He introduced me to Mr. Walter Brown, who had been a teacher at Blairsville for around 15 years with his wife teaching business courses at Union County High School. Mr. Brown gave me a list of classes, which totaled over a hundred male students. Girls were not allowed in vocational agriculture classes at that time. I was introduced to the school's canning plant, which was already in operation Tuesdays and Thursdays till fall. There was one man, Mr. Melvin Dyer, who was to help me operate the canning plant. I had taken a food processing course at UGA and in my agricultural mechanics class taken in the UGA Engineering Department. We were taught how to operate food canning glass in canning equipment.

So, on July 1, 1960, at Union County High School at the age of 22 years I began my vocational agriculture career. I had put in many hours of physical labor to have the opportunity for the responsibility I was now receiving at Union County High. I realized that some of the students I would be teaching were only four or five years younger than me. Besides running the Canning Plant, which we opened at 6:00, we worked to can all food brought into the plant. This sometimes took till 7:00 or 8:00 in the evening. I would spend long days out in the county, meeting students I was to teach and their parents. By the time school started, I had met with about all of the parents of students I would be teaching. This really paid off in student discipline. Parents told me if their son gave me any type of trouble in the classroom, just let them know. Most of the time, I was told this with their son or sons being present. The classroom tables were arranged end to end, with student around the tables. This led to great discussion opportunities, not just a lecture type class setting. It may be hard for you to believe, with things that I hear are going on with disciple problems today in 2017 teachers are having, but I had very little problems. The students knew what their parents told them: No trouble with the agriculture teacher. They were being sent to learn what I could teach them that would be very useful in their future lives.

In 1960, Vietnam and the United States went to war. We heard the names of cities of Hanoi (North Vietnam) and Saigon (South Vietnam). This turned out to be a very costly war for the U.S. Even today, we have men dying from chemicals used to defoliate the jungles of Vietnam. This was a time when young men would be drafted into military service. I was called to be given a physical exam and passed, placed in Classification (A), meaning I was placed at the top of the list to be drafted. I feel strongly that the Lord intended for me to work with high school students, teaching them many life skills. Still today in the year 2017, as over the years I taught, I had students come up to me and express thanks. For example, on August 23, 2017, when I met for lunch at the

Commerce Country Kitchen with my brothers. As we exited, a lady said hello. Her name was Daphne McDaniel. She said, "Mr. Bridges, you taught me welding in 1993 when you started the Jackson County Young Farmers Program. I went to Rome, Georgia, took a job welding—my life's work—I love it. Thanks."

My wife and I were eating lunch at Cracker Barrel when a man, a former student, approached our table saying, "Mr. Bridges, I want you to know that you launched my life's career. At Oconee County, we had the state-winning FFA string band. I knew right then that was what I wanted in my life's work. I now play in a big-time country music group. Thanks."

I did not get drafted, but there was another reason that I might not have had a chance to teach at Union County High School that I didn't know happened till sometime later.

As I have already mentioned, Mr. Mitchel had me sign a contract with the Union County Schools superintendent, but that month when he presented my name for approval to the Union County Board of Education, they wanted a local man for the job. Mr. Walter Brown contacted my district vocational agriculture supervisor, Mr. J.H. Mitchel, telling him what had happened. Mr. Brown was told for him to get the Board together for a meeting, that he wanted to meet with them on their vocational agriculture teaching strategy. At the meeting, Mr. Mitchel told the Board of Education that if they wanted a canning plant and the rest of their vocational agriculture programs funded 90 percent by state money, then they would approve Kenneth Bridges for the agriculture teacher's job. I then was fully hired to start my teaching career.

After I got a job as teacher of agriculture, Union County, Mr. Walter Nix had been teacher of agriculture next door, 17 miles east in Towns County at Hiawassee for some 20 years. Three months later at our district meeting he told a group of teachers from our mountain area that with a new vocational agriculture teacher at Union County he could take it easy for a while. However, for the next 5 years, Union County FFA did not let Towns County FFA beat them in a single contest. For my first three years at Union County, Mr. LeRoy Furgerson was my principal. He was from the Atlanta, Georgia, area. My classroom office, shop, and canning plant were behind the main high school building. The building was heated by a coal-burning boiler for steam heat. No air condition cooling for spring and summer. There were a lot of times with outside temperatures below freezing and our temperature in the classroom was never over 55 degrees. But I never remember any student complaining.

Chapter 5

Homelife and Teaching

My wife, Mary Ellen, and I were well-received in the Union County communities. We secured a small house located in the small town of Blairsville. Our landlord lived in an identical house next door. They were the Marion Parkers. Just up the street was a federal game warden. There are 90,000 acres of federal land (forest) in Union County. This county is also the location of Brasstown Bald Mountain, the highest point in Georgia, 5000 feet.

Being both of the Baptist faith, we joined the Blairsville First Baptist Church. We attended this church for the five years we lived in Blairsville. After two years, I was ordained as a church deacon. It was at this church that we got to know two fine couples that we have had a great relationship with over the years. They were Mr. and Mrs. Dick Jones and Mr. and Mrs. Steward Bloodworth.

Occasionally, Mary and I would visit on invitation some of the other churches in the mountain area. One Sunday in July, we went to a church memorial service for a veteran of foreign wars. It was a good service except that we thought the pastor should not have preached for a little over an hour. As we exited the church door, I shook the preacher's hand and told him how much we enjoyed the pretty flowers. They did have some very pretty flowers. The pastor said the flowers were placed there in honor of those who died in the service. I asked him, "Was it the morning service or the evening service?"

I joined the Kiwanis Club and had the opportunity to have my FFA members present their programs. There were a lot of good county FFA string bands and FFA quartets available. There was a lot of ability in some of my vocational agriculture students. We formed a string band and a quartet. For our FFA string band, there were the Jimmy Collins and Nathan Dyer families that lived in the Chostoe community on the south side of Union County. This was the same area where the Georgia State School Superintendent, Mr. M.D. Collins, grew up. Let me say here that we might call them hillbillies, but there are a lot of natural people talented in them there hills. Example: Mary Ellen worked in the Young Harris College admissions office, as well as working on her secretarial business degree. It was time for a Union County Junior-Senior Prom. She told me that they had just a great band that would play for the Junior-Senior Prom. The Ronnie Milsap band. They played the music for the prom. Though Ronnie Milsap was blind, he attended Young Harris College and made lots of money as a country music star—Grand Ole Opry, etc.

For my FFA quartet Kiwanis program, the Freeman family from the Lower Young Cane community supplied the talent. Larry Freeman, one of the 10th grade class members, could really play a piano. His mom helped me put a good quartet together that provided good Kiwanis Club programs. One of the strong points of our Vocational Agriculture FFA chapters was leadership and student development. In my 40 years of being involved as a vocational agriculture teacher, I would require my classes to learn the principles of conducting a group meeting—*Robert's Rules of Order Parliamentary Procedures.*

At Union County, I was teaching parliamentary procedure to my 9th grade students. We would hold our chapter FFA meetings once a month. For some reason, we had a 12th grade FFA president that had not learned well the rules of parliamentary procedures. One rule is if a discussion or a motion of action is before the group and it seems that taking a vote is in order, but discussion keeps going, as a voting member of the group you can call out "Question," which means you are ready to vote. I think our 9th grade members could tell our president was short in his knowledge of parliamentary procedures. A motion had been made, a second secured, discussion began. After a short time, one of our 9th grade FFA members called out "Question." Nothing happened. He called out "Question" again. This irritated our president, who seemed kind of mad. He loudly called out, "Give me your question, then." They really got him confused when they burst out in loud laughter. They really enjoyed their knowledge of parliamentary procedures at the future FFA meetings. However, our FFA president, Jeff Mason, got a copy of parliamentary procedures from me, studied it well, and could handle anything they brought his way. My Union County FFA Parliamentary Team put on a program for the Kiwanis Club, and Jeff Mason did a great job presiding.

My second year in the Blairsville Kiwanis Club I was elected their president. I traveled with a group to the state Kiwanis Club meeting, which was held at the state 4-H Club Camp at Rock Eagle, located at Eatonton, Georgia. I was the youngest elected at that time.

Baxter Black—a noted cowboy veteran human writer—wrote a great comment to the FFA legacy, for the newspaper *Cattle Today*. At this point, I want to share his take on the Edge of Common Sense. I quote:

"They stood before me as I was signing books in my booth at the national FFA Convention this fall in Indianapolis. The man showed his age but was still holding up. 'This is gonna be my last,' he said. I looked at him more attentively. 'How long have you been teaching vocational agriculture?' I asked. 'Thirty-eight years,' he said. There was a touch of weariness in his voice. We looked out over the sea of blue coats that surged through the huge Convention Hall. His wife took our picture. 'That's a long time to be married to an Ag teacher,' I told her, knowing the commitment a spouse must make to accommodate the late suppers, kids' projects, county fairs, field trips, night calls, weekend practices, long hours, and exhaustion that are an accepted requisite of the job description.

"She smiled and touched his elbow. 'It was worth it,' she said, and they walked away.

"The very next person extended her hand. She had a broad smile. 'If I had not seen her advisor button, it would have been easy to mistake her for one of the older students.'

"'Hi,' she said. She was excited. 'Would you sign my book?'

"'How long have you been teaching Vo Ag?' I asked.

"'This is my first year, my first time as an advisor to come to the Convention. I've been here three years before as a student. We've brought 23 kids, two in public speaking, a judging team.'

"'Thanks,' she said as she shook my hand firmly and disappeared into the crowd.

"A warm feeling slid down my back. I actually chuckled out loud. I often have occasion in my travels to remind Vo-Ag teachers of the responsibility they bear. Maybe they know it already, but I think their job is so hectic trying to balance teenage insecurities, practical real life educational subjects, and personal obligations that they don't have time to mull over the profound effect they have on their students. I believe teaching school is a noble calling. And ag teachers take it a step beyond because they are in the position to shape the professional life choices, as well as the character of pliable minds.

"They say there were 50,000 attendees to the FFA Convention. Fifty thousand kids dressed nice, behaving responsibly, treating adults politely. Not trashing hotels, yelling profanities or abusing the hospitality of our Indianapolis hosts. The locals noticed and commented over and over about what a great group the FFA was. To you folks in Indianapolis, thank you. But you can thank that advisor who has given 38 years of his life to that end. And you can expect that first-year advisor to follow in his footsteps.

"'That sea of blue coats is their legacy. They leave the world a better place. And they have a right to be proud."

The Union FFA Chapter had never shown cattle before my arrival, but I found several members interested in the prospect of showing steers. No heifers were shown during this era. After I told some students, if they did well with the five steers, I would take them to Atlanta in April to the State 4-H/FFA fat cattle show. My main problem was that there were no trimming chutes, grooming equipment, etc. Nothing. So, I built a chute with 4" by 6" timber, used saw mill belts to lift the cattle to trim their feet before state shows.

In spite of some hardships, each of my 5 years at Union County, we took show steers to the Junior Fat Cattle Show in Atlanta. At this time, when you got to the state show, not all steers were allowed to show. They had a so-called sifting judge. I remember at one show, Mr. Bruce Purdy from out of state was the sifter. Mr. Dan Daniel, Georgia Extension scientist, was with Dr. Purdy and let one of our calves in the show. Dr. Daniel told him, "Why are you letting this calf in? His feet need trimming." I spoke up with sore hands from trimming my students' calves' feet, telling them, "The feet have been trimmed." Dr. Daniel, thinking I was just one of the students, said, "Liking a foot." I did not attack Dr. Dan. Later, he learned that I was a teacher and he apologized.

In the spring of 1967 I had been teaching at Blairsville, Hiawassee, Georgia, for eight years. My wife, Mary Ellen, had graduated from the two-year college, Young Harris College, and had a job working in the Young Harris admissions office and finance office. We now had a fine baby boy named Starling Kenneth Bridges. I had, in 1962, purchased 130-acres of land where I grew up plowing mules and picking cotton. There was a lot of pine timber on this property, as well as the open land where we grew our row crops. My mom and dad had purchased acres, 13 in all, which included their house where they still lived.

From the time of purchase till 1967, I began fencing in the open land and changing its use to pastureland. Also, I would come from Union Town, down to the farm, to mark trees to be cut for pulpwood. Porter's Pulpwood Yard was located along train tracks at the low end of the town of Commerce, Georgia.

A man and his wife would cut down the trees I marked, load them onto a truck by hand—4 feet long sticks of pulpwood—and take them to the pulpwood yard. They were to get one half of the income and I would get one half of the income from the pulpwood they delivered to the pulpwood yard. Each weekend, I would come down to Porter's Pulpwood Yard at Commerce to pick up a nice-size check.

As a vocational agriculture teacher, I really liked teaching forestry in our FFA Forestry Chapter Contest. There are 10 different contest events. While teaching vocational agriculture in Oconee County for 22 years, two teams from all chapters in Northeast Georgia winners earned a trip to the state forestry FFA contest, held at State Forestry Headquarters in Macon, Georgia. I had one of those teams for 20 years while teaching at Oconee County High.

After teaching 8 years in the North Georgia mountains and wanting to move my family closer to the University of Georgia, which would make it easier to work toward a master's degree in education and also get me closer to my newly purchased cattle farm located in the Nicholson, Georgia, area. The Madison County superintendent offered me a $1,000 supplement to come to teach at Madison County High School. Also, the superintendent at Oconee County told me his Board of Education would match any deal I was offered to teach at Oconee County High.

After all being considered, my wife and I decided to take our family to Oconee County with me to teach vocational agriculture at Oconee County High School, located at Watkinsville, Georgia.

Mobile homes were becoming very popular, with a mobile home company located at Gainesville, Georgia. Paying around $11,000, Mary Ellen and I bought a 10-feet wide, 40-feet long mobile home and located it close to Mars Hill Baptist Church on a small lot already set up for a mobile home.

Mary Ellen and I had been at Watkinsville two years when, on June 26, 1969, a beautiful baby girl, whom we named Shannon Marella Bridges, was born. Mary Ellen's parents, after our two children were born, came often to see their two grandchildren. Marion and his wife, Mary Davis, lived above Braselton, Georgia, on Flowery Branch Road. They made several trips to the mountains to see us but increased their visits a lot with two grandchildren born. Also, Mom and Dad, Ralph and Lucy Bridges, increased their visits after Starling and Shannon were born. Mary Ellen and I were very proud of Starling and Shannon.

I remember taking my dad for some rides through some very narrow mountain roads. My Dad said, "Good Lord, Kenneth. Run for road commissioner and build some roads."

We had been provided most of our house furnishings while living in Blairsville, Hiawassee, so Mary Ellen and I moved our belongings to Watkinsville in two pickup truck trips. We only lost one Boston rocker on the move. Also, our new mobile home had everything installed in it that was needed for comfortable living.

Since a small boy being introduced to rabbit hunting by Dad, I had a burning passion for listening to a pack of dogs chasing a rabbit. It was a thrill for me helping my dad track down a rabbit in the snow. Our rabbit hounds were mixed breeds.

My first introduction to purebred beagles was after becoming a teacher of agriculture at Blairsville, Georgia, in 1960. A young drugstore owner, Mr. Charles Hill, was purchasing some fine gun-dog type beagles from a friend, Mr. Bill Watts of Akron, Ohio. Charles said his time was very limited and asked me to run his beagles on his farm for him. In his kennel, there was a male named Buckeye who was a 15-inch saddleback with an outstanding voice and a far-better-than-average nose. About this time, I had traded a redbone coon hound for a blue tick beagle female, pedigree unknown. I bred my beagle to Buckeye with the results being six pups. At five weeks of age, one pup died, leaving me with three males and two females.

I kept the five-beagle pack for eight years before losing two. This pack either put a rabbit in a hole or caught every rabbit they jumped. If my shotgun didn't score, these hounds didn't even break the skin on a rabbit bringing it to me, carrying the rabbit by the back of the neck. All five of these beagles would bring a caught rabbit to me.

Buckeye is now known in the Blairsville, Georgia, area as the "Million Dollar Beagle." Mr. Charles Hill tells me that he went to Lake Nottley, a lake lot auction, where he bought ten lots. Charles Hill was so impressed with

Buckeye's ability that he offered to trade Mr. Bill Watts the ten lakeside lots for Buckeye. Mr. Watts accepted this offer. Mr. Watts kept these lots, and as the North Georgia mountains developed, he recently sold them for $1 million. Never can tell what a good hound might be worth.

In my beagle pack of five was a male dog that was a duplicate of his dad Buckeye. He had all the great qualities of the "Million Dollar Beagle." I named him Buckeye and kept as much as possible of his blood in my beagles, using it to help develop my pack today that I call my "Rabbit Master Hounds."

Starting in the February 2002 issue of *The Rabbit Hunter*, I wrote six articles, stories of the Rabbit Master Hounds. Hounds men from several states came to see my hounds, including Missouri, Illinois, and Pennsylvania. You may ask, What is a Rabbitmaster? I wrote in the *National Rabbit Hunter* magazine my development of this breed, and I have included these articles in Appendix 3.

In my first year at Oconee County High, I had to get a vocational agriculture program started from the ground up, so to speak. For the previous three years, Oconee County had changed vocational agriculture teachers three times, with Mr. George Sutherland, who I would follow, being teacher for only two years. He followed three changes in the two years before, mostly anyone who would fill the vocational agriculture classroom till a full-time teacher could be found. Mr. Sutherland had a degree in agricultural economics and had been filling in as a vocational agricultural teacher till a full-time job became available in the agricultural economics field.

In my vocational agriculture senior class, I found that most of my students had not experienced much class work, and after talking with several of their parents they began to see that their full-time teacher of vocational agriculture was there to put them to work, teaching them knowledge and skills that would help them for their lives that lay ahead of them. By the time my second year of teaching at Oconee High School, I felt that at home and at school things were beginning to shape up well for my wife and myself.

One day during my summer on-farm project checks of FFA Vocational Agriculture livestock, I stopped by my home to find Mary Ellen holding our six-month-old girl, Shannon, in her arms trying hard to get an ambulance to get Shannon to the hospital as she was having convulsions. I heard her say to the operator, "Never mind. My husband is here." In a new 1970 Ford V-8 truck, we really went fast to St. Mary's for some help for our precious little daughter. Traveling down Atlanta Highway in Athens, a policeman led us at a high rate of speed, getting us to St. Mary's emergency room where our little girl got good medical help that she really needed. That was one experience Mary Ellen and I never forgot.

In Georgia, it was not until 1970 that girls could enroll in vocational agriculture. I remember my first female student was Miss Paula Whitehead. However, it wasn't long till I had girls taking agriculture, and girls in FFA in all my classes. Allowing females to enroll in vocational agriculture was an immeasurable plus value for the girls and the total vocational agriculture program. Today, year 2018, there are many highly successful women in all fields of agriculture, and this includes many highly successful lady teachers of vocational agriculture.

At this point, let me stop and mention that the world lost to death, at the age of 99, the Rev. Billy Graham, who was born in 1918. He died the week of February 18, 2018. Rev. Billy Graham's work for God is also immeasurable. Most all of our U.S. Presidents sought his advice during their terms as President.

Marilyn and I attend Commerce First Baptist Church, and in our Sunday School class Rev. Graham's death was mentioned, with our teacher telling us of him getting lost 50 years ago in Jackson County. It's known that he traveled in a limousine with others who helped him in his crusades for Christ. It seems that he went to use the restroom in Jefferson and got left by the others who thought he was in back. When they missed him, they went back and could not find him. A cab driver in town took him home to North Carolina (no cost).

My brother Ben was a captain of the Northeast Georgia State Patrol. A state trooper tells me that, after a Christian Crusade in Atlanta, Billy Graham wanted to drive the limousine home to North Carolina. It seems that going up I-85 from Atlanta he was going much too fast, so he got stopped for speeding. After checking the driver, one trooper went back to his patrol car, telling the trooper with him, "Boy, we have really stopped someone now."

"Well, who have we stopped?"

"It must be Jesus. Billy Graham is driving."

After the start of my tenth year of teaching, I was accepted into graduate school and started working on a Master's in Education Degree. This required completion of eight 5-hour credit courses and a thesis, which was really a research project good enough to be placed in the UGA main library. Starting in spring of 1970, I had two years to complete my work.

As a 12-month full-time teacher, I was given a two-week vacation, which I used for two years to work on my master's degree. Also, I took night courses that were four hours one night a week for three months. Some were held off campus, such as an advanced poultry course held at the junior college at Oakwood, Georgia.

I did two research projects. One dealt with putting four different varieties of apple twigs in peat moss and placing them in a greenhouse and checking them twice a week to see how many buds had broken open. This was to determine how many chill hours are necessary for apples to produce fruit.

For my thesis book for the UGA library, I did a research project on noise pollution in agriculture. Buying a decibel meter, I checked the noise level for all vocational agriculture mechanics lab equipment and checked the noise level for all types of farm equipment and machines being operated on the farm. I made charts recording my findings. I then had to write out explaining what I learned on noise pollution that could cause hearing loss for a person operating different agricultural equipment. A noise level of 90 recorded on a decibel meter, which a person would be exposed to when operating an agricultural piece of equipment, could cause a person hearing loss. Lots of time, noise was created above this level.

Chapter 6

Mary Ellen

When it came to writing out my results, this is where my wife, Mary Ellen, came in. She was brilliant in all levels of academics, grammar, composition, and math. No one was better than Mary Ellen. She wrote out my findings and when I would take in my work from time to time, the three doctors of education who would try to change what Mary Ellen had written to make it sound better, could not. I would laugh inside, for I knew their efforts. No matter how hard they worked, the composition always stayed as she had written them.

In the summer of 1972, my master's work was completed, and I received my Master's in Education Degree in Agriculture. Ms. Terri Hamlin, who worked with me as a vocational agriculture teacher in Oconee County was working on her doctorate. She called me and said she did not realize that I had a book in the UGA library.

Now, being in Oconee County with the help of my dad and mom living on my farm, I was able to increase my polled shorthorn herd. In 1973, I received a nice plaque for my wall – as Georgia's top shorthorn producer.

When we grew up as boys, I wrote we had no running water, no indoor toilets, and no shower in our house. However, after his four boys grew up, my father decided to add these features for more comfortable living.

My mother told me that she was in the kitchen cooking breakfast when a snake showed up. If there was anything she hated, it was a snake. Dad was in the bathroom, taking a shower. Mother hollered, "Snake in house." Now, my dad always kept a double barrel shotgun loaded on the wall. He ran out of the shower (no clothes), grabbed his gun, ran into the kitchen and asked, "Where is the snake?" Mother said, "He went up under the sink."

Dad got down on his hands and knees, looking up under the sink cabinet for the snake. Now, they kept this dog in the house. The dog ran over to where Dad was looking for the snake. He cold nosed my dad right in the rear. Both barrels of the gun went off. It blew the pipes in two. They had the plumber out for half a day, fixing them back. Never did find that snake!

The longer I live, the more I realize the impact of attitude on life. Attitude, to me, is more important than facts. It is more important than the past, than education, than money, than circumstances, than failures, than successes, than what other people think, say, or do. It is more important than appearance, giftedness, or skill. It will make or break a company ... a church ... a home. The remarkable thing is we have a choice every day regarding the attitude we will embrace for that day. We cannot change our past—we cannot change the inevitable. The only thing we can do is play on the one string we have, and that is our attitude. ... I am convinced that life is 10 percent what happens to me and 90 percent how I react to it. And so it is with you ... we are in charge of our attitudes.

Note: When a teacher has five classes of 25 students to a class, somewhere along the line, a student will be in need of an attitude adjustment, and chances are, a teacher will—

and should—for the student's good, make an attitude adjustment.

By the year 1971, I realized that progress was being made in getting my students to really get their attitudes adjusted. I would like to give two examples as evidence.

A student by the name of Tracy Carson came by my house one night to talk about his pig chain project. Tracy was very much into learning what his Vo Ag classes had to offer him and he really enjoyed showing his swine project at shows. Tracy had an older sister who had just finished high school and was planning to get married. Tracy told me, "I am really concerned about my sister getting married. You know, Mr. Bridges, she don't need to get married any more than I do, and I sure don't need to get married because I have my swine project to take care of."

No girls were allowed to take Vocational Agriculture till 1970. When girls were allowed, my first female student was Paula Whitehead. Paula showed a show steer her first year in Vo Ag. She was a very successful FFA Vo Ag student. I have included her success story in my "My Experience Raising Shorthorns in Georgia (50 Years)," which is included in Appendix 4 of this book. After Paula was such a bright addition to my program, I wondered, "Why did I have to teach for 10 years without the girls? I cannot overemphasize the great value girls play in the program.

At this time in my writing, as Easter Sunday comes this Sunday, April 1, 2018, being taught many different students of different learning abilities, I want to relate my most touching Easter story.

Jeremy was born with a twisted body and a slow mind. At the age of 12, he was still in second grade. Seemingly unable to learn, his teacher, Doris Miller, often became exasperated with him. At times, he spoke clearly and distinctly, as if a spot of light had penetrated the darkness of his brain. Most of the time, however, Jeremy just irritated his teachers. Miss Miller called his parents to come in for a consultation. As Jeremy's parents entered the empty classroom, Doris said to them, "Jeremy really belongs in a special school. It isn't fair for him to be with younger children who don't have learning problems. Why, there is a five-year gap between his age and that of the other students."

Jeremy's mother cried softly into a tissue, while her husband spoke. "Miss Miller," he said, "There is no school of that kind nearby. It would be a terrible shock for Jeremy if we would take him out of this school. We know he really likes it here."

Doris sat for a long time after they had left, staring at the snow outside the window. Its coldness seemed to seep into her soul.

She wanted to sympathize with his parents. Their only child had a terminal illness. As she pondered the situation, guilt washed over her. "Here I am complaining when my problems are nothing compared to that poor family," she thought. "Lord, please help me to be more patient with Jeremy." From that day on, she tried hard to ignore Jeremy's noise and his blank stares.

Then one day he limped to her dragging his bad leg behind him. "I love you, Miss Miller," he exclaimed, loud enough for the whole class to hear. The other students snickered, and Doris' face turned red. She stammered, "Wh-why that's very nice, Jeremy. N-now, please take your seat."

Spring came, and the children talked excitedly about the coming of Easter. Doris told them the story of Jesus, and then to emphasize the idea of new life springing forth, she gave each of the children a large empty plastic Easter egg.

"Now," she said to them, "I want you to take this home and bring it back tomorrow with something inside that shows new life. Do you understand"

"Yes, Miss Miller," the children responded enthusiastically. All except Jeremy. He listened intently; his eyes never left her face. He did not even make his usual noises. Had he understood what she had said about Jesus' death and resurrection? Did he understand the assignment? Perhaps she should call his parents and explain the project to them.

That evening, Doris' kitchen sink stopped up. She called the landlord and waited an hour for him to come by and unclog it. After that, she still had to shop for groceries, iron a blouse, and prepare a vocabulary test for the next day. She completely forgot about phoning Jeremy's parents.

The next morning, 19 children came to school laughing and talking as they placed their Easter eggs in a large wicker basket on Miss Miller's desk.

After they completed their math lesson, it was time to open the now-filled eggs. In the first egg, Doris found a flower. "Oh yes, a flower is certainly a sign of new life," she said. "When plants peek through the ground, we know that spring is here."

A small girl in the first row waved her arm. "That's my egg, Miss Miller," she called out.

The next egg shell contained a plastic butterfly which looked very real. Doris held it up. "We all know that a caterpillar changes and grows into a beautiful butterfly. Yes, that's new life, too."

Little Judy smiled proudly and said, "Miss Miller, that one is mine."

Next, Doris found a rock with moss on it. She explained that moss, too, showed life. Billy spoke up in the back of the classroom. "My daddy helped me," he beamed.

Then Doris opened the fourth egg. She gasped. The Easter egg was empty. Surely, it had to be Jeremy's, she thought, and of course he did not understand the instructions. If only she had not forgotten to phone his parents.

Because she did not want to embarrass him, she quietly put the egg aside and reached for another. Suddenly, Jeremy spoke up. "Miss Miller, aren't you going to talk about my Easter egg?"

Flustered, Doris replied, "But Jeremy, your Easter egg is empty." He looked into her eyes and said softly, "Yes, but Jesus' tomb was empty, too."

Time stopped. When she could speak again, Doris asked him, "Do you know why the tomb was empty?"

"Oh, yes," Jeremy said. "Jesus was killed and put in there. Then His Father raised Him up. And that's how Easter started."

The recess bell rang. While the children excitedly ran out to the schoolyard, Doris cried. The cold inside her melted completely away.

Three months later, Jeremy died. Those who paid their respects at the mortuary were surprised to see 19 Easter eggs on top of his casket, all of them empty.

I have in my files a supplement to *The Oconee Enterprise*, which was published for National Future Farmers of America, Week February 20-27. For the 22 years I was a teacher of Vo Ag at Oconee High School, our FFA chapter published a special edition to our county paper, telling what our FFA accomplished for that year. In the 1970-71 edition was this FFA Prayer:

"Father, we thank Thee for achievements won by the present and past generations of agriculturists. Grant unto us a belief that to live and work on a good farm or to be engaged in other agricultural pursuits is pleasant as well as challenging. May we develop leadership from ourselves and respect from others; develop our own ability to work efficiently and think clearly. Thou has entrusted us with the gift of being happy ourselves and playing square with those whose happiness depends upon us. We pray that rural America can and will hold true to the best traditions of our national life and that we can exert an influence in our homes and communities which will stand solid for our part in that inspiring task. Teach us obedience in all Thy plans for us and for mankind. In Jesus' name. Amen."

In the April-May 1970 *The Georgia Future Farmer* magazine Future Farmers exhibiting steers in the state steer show in Macon went home with their share of the winnings.

There were 268 steers shown by FFA'ers and 4-H Club members.

I mention that Paula Whitehead was my first girl to take Vo Ag FFA. In one of our special national FFA Special Edition to the *Oconee County Enterprise* in the early 1970s, girls had become a strong part of FFA. One article was written by Melanie Chandler "What News." What's new? Girls in FFA. Until 1969, that would have been something shocking. A girl in a boys' club. Although they haven't been in long, girls have made their point in where they stand. Girls have had good success in placing first in cattle shows, in land judging, and making the parliamentary procedure team. They have even become officers. They have also won trips for such things as selling the most fruit in the fruit sale. The plaque for "Star Greenhand" was also presented to a girl this year. For two years in a row, the representatives in the Parliamentary Procedure Quiz Contest have been girls. The FFA has a place in Vocational Agriculture for girls who will stand tall and proud and say, "I'm an FFA member and I am willing to support my chapter 100 percent." So come on, girls, join the crowd. Join FFA.

Back on our home front. My wife, Mary Ellen Bridges, took a job at UGA business office located on Main (Broad St), Athens, Georgia. Her parents devoted a lot of their time helping take care of Starling and Shannon while we both worked.

A member of my Vo Ag program, Steve Williams, introduced me to Mr. Allen Huston. Allen was part owner of Flower Bottling Company and had purchased a farm in Oconee County. He wanted me to help him start a shorthorn herd, which I did. Mary Ellen and I moved our trailer to his farm. Things went well. We brought the 1972 Polled Congress Grand Champion Bull at Louisville, Ky. Our story is included in my "My Experience Raising Shorthorns in Georgia."

Back row L-R: Karen Mize, Jane Jones, Sally Page, Jackie Jones, Theresa Savage   Front row L-R: Bonnie Corbin, Starr Bennett, Robbie Tiller.

In addition to my wife Mary Ellen's resume in Appendix 1, I would also like to include here a very special letter I received from C.B. Lord, Mary Ellen's boss and

Assistant Director of the Georgia Center of Continuing Education.

July 22, 1978

Dear Kenneth:

I want to take this opportunity to write you one final letter about Mary. I do not mean "final" in the sense that we will not continue to talk about her here for years to come, but final in the sense that this one is for the record.

I want you and your family, particularly Starling and Shannon, to know and remember how Mary was a member of the team here at the Center. I want your children to know about the qualities that made Mary such a valuable employee and member of that team. I want them to know about her skills, loyalty, helpfulness, caring, and above all, courage.

Mary was a highly competent and efficient person. She rose through the ranks to the very pinnacle of success available to a secretary at the Center. When she entered the hospital, she already knew that she was chosen to assume the highest position at the Georgia Center--and she reached it easily in only 2½ years. Mary had a tremendous ability and she worked constantly at improving her skills. When she was called home, she had her shorthand book with her at the hospital.

Her typing skills constantly amazed me. She could type a letter or a manuscript flawlessly and so quickly

I hardly had time to turn to other things. She gave careful thought and attention to so arranging her work, and her inventories to work flow here at the Center will stand the test of time. To Mary, her work was important. and she applied herself to it as a true calling of God.

Mary was everyday and to the end loyal to the Georgia Center, to her department, and to me. Her loyalty was expressed in a thousand ways. During our discussions with close circles of associates, we frequently discussed problems and weakness at the Center, but no outsider better say anything bad about the Center or the staff. Mary would straighten them out and quick. On the day before she passed away, she told both Director Tom Mahler and me that whatever happened in her illness, her expectation of us was that we do the right thing to see the best interests of the Georgia Center. Mary believed in the Georgia Center and was interested in seeing that what we did, we did well. Her loyalty to me personally cannot be adequately catalogued except to say that she stood steadfastly beside me during trying days, frantic situations, and difficult tasks and decisions.

One of the things that endeared her to so many was her spirit of helpfulness. She tried very hard to always be a plus, never a burden, in her relationships with people here at the Center. She would pitch in to do whatever to help no matter how menial the task. When she caught up with her own work, she would check down the hall to see if others needed her. Mary intuitively knew my weaknesses and always moved to fill in where I did not do so well. For example, she knew I did not do well with birthdays, parties, and the like, and she would move in and take charge to make sure that I was not embarrassed in these situations.

Mary found it easy to be helpful because she cared about people and honestly loved them. She cared about Mr. Mahler, and she cared about Thelma the housemaid. When she knew that she was to have surgery, she asked me to personally keep Mary Ledford, the coffee shop worker, posted on her condition because they were friends and Mary Ledford sometimes felt left out. It was that Mary cared and we all knew she cared. We knew because she let us know by the things she did and said. Only know that some people are not used to being loved as Mary loved them, and some people are never adjusted to it, but she went right on caring, slaying them with kindness, for that was Mary's way.

Finally, Mary was courageous. I have never known anyone with more courage than Mary. She walked into the lions den, faced Goliath, slew the dragon. She looked at problems as challenges, reached out and seized the rod, stood her ground and looked with confidence to the next challenge, the next day, the future. Mary knew that she was sick in a serious way, but here at the office she went about her work without any hint of dim outlook. To paraphrase William Ernest Hemingway:

In the full realm of circumstances, she did not wince, never cried out loud. Her head was blooded but not unbowed.

It matters not how straight the gate, how charged with problems the scroll, Mary was the master of her fate, she was the captain of her soul.

Mary set the example in courage for those of us here at the Center. She set a hard path to follow, for few of us have such courage.

Kenneth, Mary was a joy to work with. To Mr. Mahler, Margaret, Doris and me, she was both colleague and friend. The Center is now better in all areas because Mary walked among us.

When Mary was called home, the heartbeat of the Center stopped for a moment, so great was its loss. But Mary left with us a view of life which strengthens us and will remain with us forever.

It is our prayer that you and your family will stay close to us down through the years and call on us when we can help you as Mary helped us.

Sincerely yours,

C.B Lord

Not only did my wife Mary Ellen play a big part in the success of her office, business at her work at UGA but did a top job as a mother of Starling and Shannon, as my wife, with home management, and with teaching a group of young children at our church, Berea Baptist. Her death not only hit me and my family hard, but also she was greatly missed by many who got to know her. I remember well how the women of Berea came together and brought food to our house for Mrs. Davis and I, who now had to be all we could for 12-year-old Starling and 9-year-old Shannon who had lost a great, great mom. I now remember the hardest thing I ever did then, and still to this day, was to come home and tell my children that my wife, their mom, was called to heaven by God.

I learned a big lesson at my wife's death. My faith in God, my pastor, Rev. Claude McBride, and Rev. Verlin Reese and many friends and family helped me recover from the greatest loss I have known.

I had made no preparation for burying any member of my family. My dad, Ralph Bridges, had purchased three burial plots in the Jackson Memorial Gardens, Commerce, Ga. He donated me those three burial plots. He also had purchased two more lots in the Jackson Memorial Garden close to the Bible statues. Dad said he wanted to get my mom Lucy as close to the Bible as possible.

The summer of 1978 was a tough one, but with many close friends visiting and with the help of Mary Ellen's mom, the children and I slowly began a tough healing process.

There were many invitations to take special trips and I tried to keep Starling and Shannon involved with their church and school friends whenever possible. As for me, I tried had to take care of vocational rehab FFA summer jobs such as taking students to FFA camp, procuring show projects, and holding adult night classes, attending teacher training clinics in agriculture mechanics at the UGA College of Engineering.

A group of acquaintances in Oconee County was holding an adult Bible study for people who were now single, both men and women who had lost their mates by death.

This Bible study was being held at the home of Mrs. Marilyn Nixon whose husband, John, had died from cancer like my wife Mary Ellen. Knowing she had experienced a big loss like me, when she invited me to join the Bible study, I accepted.

In addition to the Bible study, recreation and fellowship for the group was well planned. In addition, those with children could bring them and they were well taken care of.

Starling and Shannon were being well taken care of by their grandmother, Mary Davis, who was now working a part-time lunchroom job. This made her able to be back when they got home from school.

The South Eastern Shorthorn Association was scheduled to hold their field day at our shorthorn farm in August, shortly after my wife's passing. My neighbors told me to carry out the shorthorn field day as planned. We held the field day under a big willow oak in front of my dad's and mom's house. The neighbors, with my uncle Benny Adams' directions, cooked an excellent pork barbeque meal for a large crowd of shorthorn breeders who came to see our shorthorn operation.

Chapter 7

Marilyn

The Bible says, "It is not good for man to be alone." No one knew this more than I did after I lost my beloved wife, close companion, and soul mate of 19 years. I knew that even if now she was gone that I would never stop loving her.

National Convention Biggest Ever

Nearly 250 Georgia FFA members, their advisers and state staff members were part of the largest National FFA Convention in the history of the organization. Over 20,000 registered for the four-day meeting held in Kansas City, Mo.

Vice President Nelson Rockefeller, former Georgia Governor Jimmy Carter and Cincinnati Reds baseball player Johnny Bench headed the list of distinguished speakers that appeared throughout the convention.

Several Georgia FFA members and chapters were recognized for outstanding achievement, and others played an important role in the convention proceedings.

Serving as Georgia's official delegates this year were State FFA President Gary Black from Commerce; State FFA Secretary Charles III, Camilla and former State FFA Vice President David Hawks, Commerce.

Four Georgia FFA advisers were among 92 teachers of agriculture from 35 states to receive the Honorary American Farmer Degree, the highest honor the organization bestows on non-members. Selected for their years of service to FFA, the number of award winning FFA members who have developed under the leadership and the records of achievements posted by their local chapters were Paul S. Hosmer, Chattooga High School, Menlo; Henry A. Moses Jr., Montgomery County High School, Mt. Vernon; Henry R. Neal, Troup Senior High, LaGrange and Homer Patterson, Tift County High, Tifton.

Dr. Curtis Corbin Jr., state supervisor of agricultural education and state FFA advisor, received a Distinguished Service Award for his outstanding contributions to the organization.

Participating in this year's National FFA Band and Chorus were five Georgians. Band members were Rusty Freeman, Canton; Randall Morris, Uvalda and Brantley Ricks, Soperton. Chorus members included Debra Johnson, Lobburn, and James Webb, Boston.

Ocone Co. FFA President Greg Carson and advisor Kenneth Bridges accepted the State Chapter Achievement award for the Oconee Co. chapter at the State FFA Rally.

Oconee Is Top Chapter

During the past year, when winners of various FFA awards programs are announced, there has been one FFA chapter consistently represented—Oconee Co. So, it's no wonder that this chapter was selected as Georgia's top FFA chapter for 1974-75 at the State Rally in Macon.

As their award for being selected as State Chapter Achievement winner, the Oconee FFA received $100 and a plaque from the F. W. Woolworth Co., co-sponsor of the awards program with the Georgia Association of FFA.

What did this chapter do to earn the coveted chapter achievement award? Here are just a few of its accomplishments.

• The chapter received a National Gold Emblem Chapter Award at the National FFA Convention. This is the top chapter award in the organization.

• The National FFA Week publicity award went to Oconee. As part of their activities, members published a special edition of the county newspaper.

• Georgia has been represented in the National Dairy products contest by a judging team from Oconee. The team earned a Silver Emblem both years.

• A representative of this chapter placed first in the district public speaking contest for two consecutive years.

• The chapter forestry team won the area contest and earned the right to participate in the State Forestry Field Day.

• The chapter placed second in the district quartet and string band contests, and third in the parliamentary procedure.

• A member of the Oconee Co. chapter served as State FFA Vice President last year.

• In livestock events the chapter exhibited 42 head of beef cattle and 26 head of swine at eight major shows throughout the State and earned several champion and reserve champion awards as well as placings in showmanship.

January, 1976

Page 3

However, I was very lonely, but slowly I realized I must carry on with my life as God had plans ahead for me as a father of Starling and Shannon and teaching high school vocational agriculture at Oconee County High School.

Also, to make sure that a strong FFA program now going strong would not suffer from my loss. An example of our strong FFA program was that Oconee FFA chapter was picked as Georgia's top chapter for the 1974-75 school year. Oconee County FFA president Greg Carson and advisor Kenneth Bridges accepted the state chapter achievement award for the Oconee County chapter at the state FFA rally.

I attended Marilyn's Bible study fellowship regularly and talked with her at school as David and Melanie were top students in my vocational agriculture FFA program. I became very interested in asking her for a date, which I did and she accepted. I want to say here that there were several other men who wanted to get a date with Marilyn Nixon.

On our first date, I took her out for supper at the Western Sizzlin' Steakhouse located on Baxter Street in Athens, Ga. We really got to know each other better. I learned that Marilyn mostly grew up in High Point, Mt. Pilot, N.C. I quickly learned she was a woman who shared my life values and was a joy to be with. I did not want this date to be the last one with her.

Marilyn had earned her RN degree from Berea College in Kentucky. After John's death, she took a doctor's office job with Dr. Duboise who was one of Athens, Ga.'s most respected medical doctors.

All during the fall and winter months, Marilyn and I began spending time together. Marilyn took me to meet her family in North Carolina, and I took her and introduced her to members of my family.

In November, I had been chosen to represent the Georgia State Vocational Agriculture Teacher's Association at the National Vocational Agriculture Teachers Association Conference, to be held in Dallas, Texas. I flew out of Atlanta, Ga., on Thursday, attended the convention that lasted till lunch the following Monday, then my plane flight from Dallas to Atlanta arrived at 9:00 EST. Since it was Monday night and I knew it was Bible study night at Marilyn's, I decided to stop by her house to check on things. Marilyn's daughter, now sixteen, had not come home and I found one of the men had stayed on after to study to make sure she was okay. Need I say that I let him go, and I made sure Melanie got home, and it was great to see the special lady that I was very fond of.

March came, 1979, and Marilyn Nixon and I had many dates throughout the fall and winter months. I now knew that I had learned to love Marilyn and that she would be a great wife for me and mother for my children. I now knew I needed to propose marriage. It was the middle of March when I called Marilyn and asked if I could stop by her house and she said yes. I stopped by Foster's Jewelry Store in Athens, Ga., where I bought her a beautiful diamond ring. Back in 1979, with no cell phones, only land lines, I had to wait a long time to call her from Nicholson, Ga., to tell her good night at bedtime. Now it was time to see if she would consent to being my wife. Then we could say goodnight together. In the dining room of Marilyn's home, I proposed, asking if she would consent to marrying me, holding her in my arms, looking into that beautiful face and eyes. She said, "Yes, I will marry you." Quickly, I reached into my pocket, retrieved the ring that I had bought at Foster's, and slipped it on her finger. It was a perfect fit. Knowing it would take time to well plan the wedding, we set June 15, 1979.

As I write, it is now the week of June 15, 2018, and this will be our 39th year together. Remember back to 1977 when Marilyn came to my office at Oconee County High School checking on her children at school when out of nowhere a voice said to me, "She could be your wife," I have been blessed by God with two wives which no man has been better blessed. I want to thank the Lord for helping me, blessing me, allowing me to have Mary Ellen Davis and Marilyn Virginia Cook as my life soul mates.

In making our plans for our wedding, putting our two families together—two boys and two girls, all of different ages—we felt we needed a bedroom for each of them. Since I was teaching vocational agriculture in Oconee County, we would make Marilyn's home our home as a new family dwelling. But there was a problem!

When John and Marilyn Nixon decide to move their family to Oconee County, they bought a five-acre tract of land just off Hwy 441, known as the Puritan Mill property. Puritan Mill is located on both sides of Barber Creek and was zoned industrial. John and Marilyn bought the mill superintendent's house with their five acres, coming down and including the mill dam at Barber Creek. This pond gave a place for David and Melanie to fish and swim.

When we decided we would need to add two new bedrooms to the house, we were told not to do this by the Oconee County Planning Board, stating that the house was zoned for industrial, thus a residential addition would not be lawful. However, explaining our need after our marriage, the board changed the property to residential. The Oconee County paper ran a story about Marilyn's and my problem, they made a big emphasis on the fact that love won out in the end.

We hired a builder, and by May two new rooms, a hallway, and a bathroom were added. A lot of other marriage plans took place in April and May. We picked Milledge Avenue Baptist Church as the location for our wedding and Pastor Claude McBride agreed to perform the wedding ceremony.

Several of my fellow lady teachers at school would tease me, stating that they didn't think I could pass the marriage blood test. But I did. A large crowd attended.

For our honeymoon, we took a boat cruise to the Caribbean, stopping at Puerto Rico, going down as far as St. Thomas and St. John Islands. I remember Marilyn and I sitting under a coconut tree beside a very clear, green ocean.

Our children were well taken care of while we were on our trip. Neither of us had ever seen a large sea vessel. I was amazed that it always seemed to be moving slowly. Marilyn and I were well-pleased with our honeymoon.

Grandma Davis still had her home on Flowery Branch Road, and she moved back there shortly after we moved all the things headed for me, Star, and Shannon to our new home in Oconee County. However, it was not long after she moved back to her home on Flowery Branch Road that Mary met Marrion Pinnell at her church. He had lost his wife to death. He had several children who attended the church who thought Mary would make him a good wife. Marrion and Mary starting dating. The love bug took over, and they married and took a honeymoon trip to Hawaii. They moved into Marrion's home, where they had a good life together till his death and her death.

As far as my Vo Ag FFA adult program, it had grown to a two-teacher department in the early part of the 1970s. As teacher, I was joined by Dennis Clarke who was to get a horticulture greenhouse agriculture program started. Dennis Clarke had his master's degree but needed to get at least three years' experience in order to obtain a doctor's degree in Agricultural Education. After teaching three years, he went back and obtained his Doctor of Agricultural Education Degree. Then he was hired as Oconee County's vocational director.

Taking over the horticulture as our new teacher of agriculture was Mrs. Pam Stratton. Pam grew up in upstate New York and did her Bachelor of Science Agriculture Degree at UGA. Oconee County High School was her first teaching job, and she was a great help with our Oconee County FFA program, as well as doing a great job with our Vo Ag horticultural program Pam's husband, Chris, was finishing his four-year college degree, using an ROTC scholarship, which meant that he would have to pay it back by spending time as an officer in the military. Chris and Pam purchased some land just beyond the Oconee Country line on the Morgan County side of the river. They built a home, where they live today, 2018, with their two boys.

Keeping all the FFA National Week editions we published in our local Oconee County paper, there were many outstanding FFA chapter accomplishments, which I would like to include in my book.

Chapter 8

Family

Our son David finished his senior year and graduated from high school in 1979 and entered West Georgia College. David had worked many grocery store jobs all during high school. This really taught him well, as did working part-time jobs in his college years, as well as after college. Read his accomplishments in my cattle section.

Our daughter Melanie finished her senior year, graduated from high school in 1981 and entered UGA, living on campus. Melanie's major was graphic arts. All during high school, she was a top student in art classes, painting beautiful pictures, some which now hang on walls in our home on Richard Bridges Road. Melanie now has a top position at Southern Graphics Systems, Atlanta, Ga. Mr. Roger Bail, Melanie's high school English teacher, told me that Melanie took a back seat to no one in mental ability.

Our son, Starling, graduated from high school in 1985. He had talked with an Army recruiter about entering the Armed Forces and wanted to be part of the Intelligence, and later the FBI, as his service to his country. He was told that he could do that if he would enlist in the Army since he had an excellent high school grade record.

I remember the day his mom and I took him to the Athens Greyhound Station to go to Fort Jackson, S.C., for basic training. It was hard to see him go, but it was his life, and with all four of our children, we let them choose their life's work. Starling was an excellent member of Vo Ag FFA contest teams. I remember one judge of an FFA Parliamentary Procedure contest told me that my son really did an excellent job with his part of our team. He said, in fact, that he was one of the best of anyone in all the FFA Parliamentary Procedure teams he had judged.

However, after about a year in the Army, he realized they were not placing him where he was promised. Starling went to the military law library, studied what he could do to get out of the Army, built a strong case that the Army did not give him what they promised, and won an honorable discharge. He was told by his superior officers that he needed to become a lawyer because they never knew of anyone to get done just what he had accomplished.

Starling came home, enrolled at the University of Georgia, and made the dean's list. Also, he had gotten into bicycle racing in high school and made the UGA bicycle racing team. Starling has his Bachelor of Science degree and a Master of Science degree in psychology. He is Director of the Hickey House drug recovery center and a counselor for DESAC.

Our daughter Shannon finished high school in 1987. After a year in college, she became engaged and married Mitch Lay, whom she dated during high school. Mitch was a local Oconee man who was enlisting, as his two brothers had done, in the Armed Forces.

Mitch and Shannon were married June 26, 1988, which was also Shannon's birthday. The wedding was held at Watkinsville First Baptist Church. Six days later, our first grandchild was born, July 2, 1988. Garnette Smith was born to Melanie and Tim Smith. My wife, Marilyn, and I had a lot of great family events the summer of 1988.

Mitch Lay, with our daughter Shannon, was in the Armed Forces for four years. They were stationed in several countries, with the biggest being Italy. Shannon liked animals, which included cats. She had two cats from Italy that she sent home.

All during their four years in service, Shannon worked on her Bachelor of Art Degree in Business, and shortly after their service, Shannon finished her Master of Arts Degree in Business.

While in the Armed Forces, stationed at Fort Knox and Ft. Campbell in Kentucky, a daughter, Melinda "Mendi" Ellen Lay, was born November 1, 1993. On July 20, 1998, a son, Andrew Mitchell Lay, was born.

Shannon and Mitch moved back to Oconee County and built their home. Mitch enrolled at UGA and got an advanced degree in computer science. He took a job with a large company, where he still works in 2018. With her degree in accounting, Shannon procured a job at the UGA business department, where she was in charge of handling the Student Hope Scholarships between Georgia and the University of Georgia. Like her mother, Shannon quickly moved to a head position in the University of Georgia Business Department.

It has been said that political blood runs both deep in the Bridges' blood and the Rogers' blood. My grandfather, Ben Rogers, in 1936, was running for political office in Madison County, in the county seat of Danielsville, Ga.

Grandpa Ben won, but he took the flu and passed away in the fall of 1936. Also, on December 22, 1936, my dad and mom, Ralph Bridges and Lucy Rogers, were united in marriage. I never got to know my grandpa Ben Rogers, as I was born November 8, 1937. I have a picture of Mom and Dad taken the summer of 1937. Many who have looked at this picture have told me my mom was carrying her first-born son, Kenneth Rogers Bridges.

Now my three brothers, as well as myself, have been elected to political offices. To retire from teaching school in Georgia with full retirement benefits requires some 30 years, which I completed in the year 1990. At this time, a new Oconee County high school was to be built. Looking at the plans of the proposed agriculture department I was not pleased with what I saw. It was election time for county offices in Oconee County. Our superintendent, Mr. Sammy Sanders, was retiring. Mrs. Debra Harden ran and won the superintendent office. I ran and won the job as chairman of

Oconee County Board of Education. Mr. Scott Berry ran for Oconee County sheriff and won that office, an office he still holds today in 2018.

While I was serving as Oconee County chairman of the Board of Education, my brother Ben was serving as a state representative for Habersham and White Counties. Zell Miller was governor of Georgia. I was called to the State Capital during a session of state legislation and given a citation for services as chairman of Oconee County Board of Education, signed by the governor. It hangs on my living room wall.

By the year 1990, Oconee County was starting to increase heavily in population. Subdivisions had grown up heavily around our home on 441. A strip mall with a Golden Pansley store was in front of our property. The county now had a new high school second to none in the state, a new middle school on Malcomb Bridge Road. I was now pleased with the vocational agriculture department facilities at the high school.

As chairman of the Oconee County School System Board of Education, I was involved with many very important school issue decisions that were made. At this time, at the location of the new high school, a county civic center was built. My son-in-law Mitch Lay stated to me one day, "Kenneth, you had an impact on Oconee County. Your name is on a plaque that hangs on the wall of the civic center." The old high school became a middle school and my two grandchildren Mendi and Drew Lay had a great teacher of vocational agriculture and I had the opportunity as their granddad, a chance to take them for their class work to show two heifers for class talks each gave about cows. I was very proud of them. Both did a great job in their class assignments.

At the new high school, two of my former Vo Ag students became agriculture teachers, M.C. Stan Mitchell and Sidney Ball. Also, at this point, I want to pay tribute to a lady I had the privilege of working with in the Vo Ag at Oconee High School after Mrs. Stratton. Terri Hamlin joined me as teacher of vocational agriculture in the early 1980s. Oconee County was her first teaching assignment, but she took over the great horticulture program Mrs. Stratton had started. The students really enjoyed her classes. She managed student discipline and had students really involved in class and the greenhouse projects. She really learned quickly the job of teaching Vo Ag to high school students. The Lord really blessed me when he sent Miss Hamlin my way.

After I had taught my last year at Oconee, Miss Hamlin completed her doctor's degree and took a job teaching horticulture as a member of the District III Office of Vocational Agriculture, located on the UGA campus and, later, Terri's classes at UGA and finished her teaching career with the Georgia Department, starting a very successful program in which farmers grow and supply food to local school lunch rooms.

Also, let me add that over all the years since 1990, Terri Hamlin has always sent me on my birthday a beautiful card with good warm words of encouragement.

We were a great team working at Oconee High School as teachers of agriculture. Thanks so much, Terri!

I want to add that serving in the district agriculture office, I have had several former Oconee County agriculture students: Mr. Stan Mitchell, district supervisor; Mr. Bland Marable, district forestry; program, FFA contest director; Mr. Sidney Bell, district agriculture mechanics program.

I am also very proud of my nephew, John Thomas "Chip" Bridges, who soon will finish his Vo Ag teaching career. Chip was a very successful high school agriculture teacher. He was promoted to the North Georgia District Office, then on to Georgia State Director of Vocational Agriculture Education, located in Atlanta, Ga. Chip has done an outstanding job as state Vo Ag director. Thanks, Chip.

Chapter 9

Jackson County Young Farmers Program

After 22 years teaching Vo Ag in Oconee County, 5 years in Union County, Blairsville, 3 years in Towns County, Hiawassee, I had served a total of 30 years. This made it now possible for me to retire with full teaching benefits.

However, I was contacted by Mrs. Janet Adams, supervisor of Vocational Education, Jackson County High School, telling me that her two agriculture teachers, Mr. Phillip Todd and Mr. Ken Bray, along with herself, felt a strong need to establish a full-time Young Farmers Program for Jackson County.

After consulting with my wife, Marilyn, I told Mrs. Janet Adams that I would not retire but give them two years of my service, establishing the Jackson County Young Farmers Program.

Starting with July 1, 1990, I became the first full-time Young Farmers teacher for Jackson County. My office was located at the new Jackson County High School, Jefferson, Georgia.

Since I was the newest member of the vocational family, I was assigned to open up each morning at 7:00 a.m. To do this meant getting up at 5:00 a.m., taking care of our home in Oconee County and opening up at 7:00. Which I did with no problem.

One of my reasons for agreeing to start a Young Farmers Program in Jackson County was that this was back on my home turf. Going all my high school years at

Commerce High School, I also considered Madison County my home turf. The place of my birth, Rogers Mill, was home of a large number of members of both my mom's and dad's families.

I was told by many people, after I finished college, not to take a job close to home and they would give me many different locations. I was looking forward to the challenge. I also liked my calling from God to become a teacher of agriculture and nowhere in my Bible did I find that I should retire from His calling.

As agriculture teacher, one of our first jobs was to move from the old high school on Gordon Street, to the new high school, ready by the time school started. A lot of manpower was needed, so Mr. Todd, Mr. Bray, and I helped move some of the vocational departments to the new high school.

Some of you may ask: What is the job of a Young Farmers agriculture teacher? Let me first say that it doesn't only apply to being of a young age. It applies to anyone who needs help in their agriculture enterprise. Mrs. Janet Adams, my vocational supervisor, assigned me a first-period high school class at the new high school. In this class I was to teach Vo Ag high school students electric arc welding, oxygen acetylene mig and tig welding, electrical wiring, and many other agricultural-type skills in agricultural mechanics.

My agricultural classroom was located adjacent to the agricultural mechanics lab. In my job, I was also to organize adult classes and teach adult classes on the topics listed above, as well as livestock production or any other agricultural enterprise where needed.

Like in FFA (Future Farmers, Agriculturists of America), there is a state Young Farmers organization with state officers, chapter officers in counties, where a Young Farmer program exists.

Our district state livestock consultant, Mr. Billy Moss, also lived in Jackson County, along with the other help I have listed above. Soon I had a good list of contacts to make toward holding an organizational meeting to set up our Jackson County Young Farmers Chapter. Also, I attended and joined the Jackson County Cattlemen's Association. If you read my section on breeding shorthorn in Georgia for 50 years, you know that by this time the poultry industry in Northeast Georgia was well-developed to one of the largest in our nation. I encouraged my Vo Ag high school students to get a college degree in poultry science. If they did that, they could live in Northeast Georgia and have a rewarding job in agriculture. Two of my former students were Tony Townly and Zack McElroy, who now own the Zacksby's restaurant franchise.

To make my contacts meant that I would have to drive lots of miles throughout Jackson County. I thus needed an economical vehicle. At the Athens Nissan dealership I was able to find a 1984 King Cab Nissan twin cab small pickup truck. This truck had 85,000 miles on it, but it had been well taken care of, so I purchased it for $6,500. I might add that it had Datsun on the tailgate, as Nissan had bought Datsun that year. This truck allowed me to get my contacts made and work each day with my Young Farmers in a very economical, efficient way.

At the time I was forming the Jackson County Young Farmers, my wife's dad, Eugene Cook, now in his eighties, had moved in with us in our home in Oconee County. Mr. Cook had spent his lifetime traveling, tuning pianos. He never had a music lesson, but he became famous in the Mt. Pilot, North Carolina, area for making pianos sound their best. In the *Andy Griffith Show*, "Aunt Bee played a piano turned by Gene Cook.

In the fall of 1990, we held our first Young Farmers chapter meeting and elected our chapter officials.

President: Dwight Cooper

Vice President: Tim Brooks

Secretary: Steve Childs

Treasurer: Gregg Pittman

Reporter: Brant McMullan

Sentinel: David Mooney

I was very pleased with the way my vocational supervisor did her job. In fact, I considered her the very best in my teaching agriculture career. Mrs. Janet Adams would get all of the vocational departments together once a month. She always had plans with how, working together, we could make Jackson County High School Vocational Department tops. She showed us how, by working together, everyone in the department could do their job better. I found the typing teachers were a big help to getting out my adult materials.

Since Jackson County had a large number of both purebred and commercial cattle, a great amount of my Young

Farmer work was in helping on the farms with managing their herds. This also would be going to their farms on Saturdays, working a cattle herd, there being a large number of purebred cattle herds of different breeds.

Two things that the newly formed Jackson County Young Farmers saw a need for were establishing a county purebred breeder association and establishing a Jackson County Young Farmers replacement heifer sale. Both of these were very successful, with the help of Mr. Billy Moss, our registered purebred breeder, who held a class on problems occurring when raising purebred cattle.

Each year, the state Young Farmers will hold a Young Farmers convention and tour farms in different parts of Georgia. In 1990-91, Jackson County Young Farmers had a tour of farms in Southeast Georgia. In 1992, we went to Columbus, Georgia, and took farm tours. As I write this in 2018, I am proud to say that this year's Georgia Young Farmers Tour was Jackson and Madison Counties. In Jackson County, the full-time Young Farmers program is very strong. It is a great inspiration to me that God led me to get it started.

By the May closing of the 1992 school year, I had completed 32 years of teaching vocational agriculture. A retirement banquet was held in my honor. It was put together by many and attended by many.

Note: Thirty-one people wrote a typed page for the scrapbook from Union, Town, Oconee, and Jackson Counties, telling that my Vo Ag teaching had been a blessing to them. Some of these are in Appendix 1. I have included a few photos here.

In 1993-94, I was elected President of the Jackson County Cattlemen Association. This also was the year that my dad, Ralph Bridges' first cousin (also Ralph Bridges) was elected to serve as President of the Georgia State Cattlemen

Association. We started giving our county churches a chance to serve our meals. We would be giving them a chance with us getting a sponsor to pay for our meals, with money going to the churches. Also, we would have each member who came and ate at our meetings put in two dollars. In the spring, when time to hold our local Junior Jackson County Cattle Show, we would have a good pot of prize money.

My cousin Ralph would travel the state, visiting local cattle shows. I invited Ralph to be the guest speaker at a Nicholson church. He was, at one time, President of the National Angus Cattlemen Association. It was a great program, with large groups of Jackson County cattlemen attending.

As I am writing this, it is August 2, 2018. On August 2, 2016, I lost my daughter Shannon and Starling's sister to cancer at the age of 47 years. She fought a hard fight, with the help of her Aunt Kathy and her brother Starling. If you read my cattle section, you will find her as a small girl leaning on a shorthorn cow, with her brother milking the cow. You will also find where Starling wrote and delivered her eulogy.

At this point, I would like to include Shannon's obituary that appeared in the *Athens Banner* newspaper. Her mother died at 38 years. Both made outstanding accomplishments while on earth, and they are now together in heaven with their Lord.

Shannon Marella Bridges Lay(1969 - 2016)

It is with great sadness the family of Shannon Marella Bridges Lay announces her passing after a heroic battle against cancer. Shannon, wife of Mitch and mother to daughter, Mendi and son, Drew, passed early Tuesday morning in her home in Watkinsville, GA at the age of 47. Shannon was born on June 26th, 1969 in Athens, Georgia and moved with her family to Oconee County in 1979. She graduated from Oconee County High School in 1987; she obtained her Bachelor's degree from Augusta College in 1996 then went on to earn her MBA from Brenau College. She was a 20- year employee of The University of Georgia, Accounts Payable Department. Shannon was also a long-time member of Watkinsville First Baptist Church where she cherished her church family.

Shannon leaves behind her husband of 28 years, Mitch age 48, born in Athens, Georgia and two children, Mendi and Drew. She is preceded by her mother, Mary Ellen Davis Bridges, her mother-in-law, Nora Melinda Davis, and her grandmother, Mary (Granny) Davis. She is survived by her father Kenneth Bridges and his wife Marilyn, her brother Star Bridges, her sister Melanie, her brother David and their families. She is also survived by in-laws Johnny, Jay, and Mark Lay and their families and many others who both influenced her life and were equally influenced by her including her Aunt Kathy, Qizhe Zeng (Jerry), life-long high school friends and co-workers.

Those who had the privilege of knowing Shannon will remember her smile and charm, as she blessed all those who crossed her path. Her reputation of grace, humor and faith defined her, and her quick wit always improved the moods of those around her. She put her family and faith before everything, loved her Lord Jesus with all her heart, and naturally put others before herself no matter what she was going through. She fought hard to beat cancer, and was the epitome of strength throughout the fight. Shannon was at peace with what was to come, and her family and friends take comfort in that along with the fact that she knew she would be going home to her Savior.

Visitation with the family will be at Lord and Stephens West on Friday, August 5th, from 6 to 9 pm with services held at Watkinsville First Baptist Church on Saturday, August 6th, at 10 am. Shannon will be laid to rest at Oconee Memorial Park, 2370 Hwy 53 in Watkinsville, GA. Her love for animals and her battle against cancer continues; therefore in lieu of flowers, the family request donations to the ASPCA, 424 E. 92nd St., New York, NY 10128 or The American Cancer Society , 6500 Sugarloaf Pkwy #260, Duluth, GA 30097.

Lord and Stephens, West is in charge of arrangements.

www.lordandstephens.com

1969 - 2016

LORD & *Stephens*

Funeral Home
Lord & Stephens Funeral Home - West Chapel
1211 Jimmy Daniel Road Watkinsville, GA 30677
(706) 549-3342

Published in Athens Banner-Herald on Aug. 4, 2016

Chapter 10

Life After Retirement

Back in 1981, Marilyn and I sold our house and the tract of land at our farm at Nicholson, Ga., where the house was located. We kept the major part of the farm for raising our registered shorthorn cattle herd which, at that time, numbered about 50 head. As I mentioned, at our Watkinsville home we had become surrounded by commercial, residential development.

I would drive up from our home on White Oak Drive to check the cow herd with Marilyn's dad, now living with us, coming with me. Marilyn and I had already talked about building us a house on our farm. On one trip to the farm, I saw a for-sale sign at our house with a tract of land we sold back in 1981. We were able to buy back our house and land and, after a year of additions, updating, and changing things to how we liked and wanted our dream home to be, in May 1993, we started moving from Oconee County to our farm. Mr. James Hunter, one of my students in Oconee County who became a Vo Ag teacher for several years then joined his brother who had a very successful construction business, did the work for us. Mr. Hunter also purchased our house and land in Oconee County and built UGA student apartments, making his purchase from us very profitable to him.

I set to work after our move, setting up a cattle barn where I could get cattle ready for shows. I cleared more land at our house site, then set up fencing for show cattle to run.

We lost Mr. Eugene Cook October 1992 at age 88 from lung problems.

In the years that followed, I used my barn to sponsor FFA and 4-H students who needed a place to get to have a show calf for an FFA or 4-H school project. If you read the shorthorn section of my writing, you will see the pictures of some of the students. Today, August 11, 2018, I am working with the teachers throughout the state of Georgia, as well as county agents with students on their 4-H and FFA cattle projects. I am still working hard with my shorthorn breeding program to sell students quality polled shorthorn heifers and steers for showing at a sensible price.

After our move to our farm, we moved our church membership back to Berea Baptist Church from Living Word Baptist, Bogart, Ga. For the next 8 years, Marilyn and I taught in the church Sunday School classes, worked with the church youth groups, and Marilyn sang in the church choir and I served on the deacon board. In 1998, we decided to move our church letters close to our home to Nicholson Baptist Church. This church was in the process of building onto the present church, which turned out to be a very Christian experience and a place to worship God. Marilyn and I always tried to stay close to the Lord and seek His protection and divine guidance in our lives. We also tried to bring our children up in a good Christian environment. I remember our daughter, Shannon, saying to me one time, "Dad, I am sure glad that I was raised up in a strong Christian home." Shannon and her husband, Mitch, have passed on to their children, Mendi and Drew, strong, moral, Christian teaching. Two times in my life, my God stepped in. Read about my bull attack in my shorthorn section of my writing.

The doctors told the nurses that I was going to die from my kidney cancer in in 2005. My God stepped in and saved my life. I have good health today August 11, 2018.

After my retirement from full-time teaching, I had more time to enjoy my two hobbies, running rabbits with my Rabbitmaster hounds, and fishing. However, Mrs. Janet Adams and administrators in education had started a six-county charter school, held at night for students who had to drop out of school for different reasons. The counties consisted of Jackson, Madison, Stephen, Oconee, Clark, and Barrow. Since a lot of the students had daytime jobs, it was set up as a credit for job work done and class work completed for a high school diploma. The school was completed as a regular high school, plus things like a nursery for students with small children. Mrs. Janet Adams was to serve as the school principal.

To start with, the school was held at the new Jackson County High School. Classes were held for two hours, from 8:30 to 10:30 p.m., Monday-Friday nights. I was asked to teach a class in the different types of welding, electrication, wiring, etc., and check the students to which I was assigned on their day work jobs. After my two years of teaching charter school, it was moved to the Gordon Street School Center, starting at 6:30 p.m. and ending at 8:30 p.m. This school in which I taught for 8 years was very successful to students. Most graduated with high school diplomas.

It was really rewarding to me to have many students that I taught, some who had been to student boot camp, tell me how much I meant to them in life using the knowledge that I taught them in night school classes.

Mrs. Janet Adams gave us teachers a framed motto that I hang on the wall in my home. It was a quote from The Story of Christa McAuliffe, the teacher who died when the space shuttle exploded: "I touch the future. I teach." In my retirement from years of teaching I have learned that this is so true.

One of the big problems people have is making good choices in life. Mrs. Adams and I agreed that the eighth and ninth grade is a level in their education that students need help in making good choices.

I volunteered to teach some classes at different eighth and ninth grade levels at Jackson County Middle Schools. Mrs. Adams secured the teaching choices and materials, and I would go when asked.

Also, Mrs. Beth Bray, principal at Commerce grammar school, asked me to teach some of their students how to call a pig. I did, and after two hours of teaching hog calling to half the grammar school, two days later, I could hardly talk. I know that I was effective in teaching pig calling. A year later, I was walking down a street in Commerce when a little boy called out, "Momma, Momma, there's the pig man."

Chapter 11

Late-Life Experiences That Impacted My Life in the 21st Century

I remember well when the year 2000 arrived. Marilyn and I had often visited a little store and restaurant in our small town of Nicholson called Lester's. It was at this store that we got to know lots of the people I had known as a young boy and many that had moved to the area.

Two men who were brothers, Olin and Frank Whitehead, lived on Stapher Road off New Kings Bridge Road. They were born and still lived in the same house all their lives, and they were now in their late seventies. Frank and Olin never married but had close kin, the Palmers and the Brooks, living close by. After church, Marilyn and I would lunch and visit with them. We were really impressed with their life tales they would tell us.

Olin told us that when he was a young boy, he was operated on for an appendicitis by Dr. Amory Rogers, my Grandpa Ben's brother. He said Dr. Rogers told them he would do the operation on the kitchen table at their house. They were to close all the blinds at the windows, kill all the flies, and disinfect the table. Olin said he came through the removal of his appendix operation fine, a greater result than ending up dead. How would you like any operation in the above manner?

Lester and his wife, Betty, always had a good group of customers for breakfast and lunch, both local and people traveling down U.S. Highway 441, which is a major U.S. highway that runs from Ohio through Florida.

In the Nicholson community, there are many Smith families. Marilyn and I have gotten to know a large number of them. I believe Nicholson should have been named Smithville.

At Lester's, I had many experiences. One day, I was talking to a young boy whose dad I had known. I asked him how old his dad was. He answered, "Ten years old." I replied, "No, that is your age." The boy told me his dad was not a dad till he was born.

My little granddaughter was sitting on my lap, and I was reading her a story. From time to time, she would take her eyes off the book and reach up and touch my wrinkled cheek. By and by, she was alternately stroking her own cheek and then my cheek. Finally, she spoke, "Granddaddy, did God make you?"

"Yes, sweetheart," I answered. "God made me a long time ago."

"Oh," she said. "Then Granddaddy, did God make me, too?"

"Yes indeed, honey," I assured her. "God made you just a little while ago."

"Oh," she said, feeling our faces again. Then she observed: "God's getting better at it now, isn't He?"

In our home, we have a little black dog named Wiggles. Wiggles is of the Stephens breed. In all my life, I have never had a dog that better met what a person could ask for in any manner than Wiggles. Read her story in my dog section. Then read "The Little Black Dog," which I am including at this point, and you will read our story of Wiggles.

The Little Black Dog

By Elizabeth Gardner Reynolds

I wonder if Christ had a little black dog

All curly and wooly like mine;

With two long silky ears and a nose round and wet,

And two eyes, brown and tender, that shine.

I am sure, if He had that that little black dog

Knew right from the first, that He was God;

That he needed no proof that Christ was divine

And just worshiped the ground where He trod.

I'm afraid that he hadn't because I have read

How He prayed in the garden alone

For all of His friends and disciples had fled

Even Peter, the one called a stone.

And oh, I am sure that the little black dog

With a heart so tender and warm

Would never have left Him to suffer alone

But creeping right under His arm

Would have licked the dear fingers, in agony clasped

And counting all favors but loss

When they took Him away, would have trotted behind

And followed Him right to the cross.

Around the first part of the year 2000, the U.S. Department of Transportation decided that they would widen U.S. 441 into a four-lane highway, which they did. Back at Marilyn's and my home in Oconee County, 441 also ran by. Many people, there as well as here in the Nicholson area, thought they could dictate to the U.S. government where they would build the new 441, four-lane highway.

However, even though a large number tried hard to stop the U.S. Department of Transportation from widening the road, the road was widened all along the two lanes. I remember one meeting on discussion of where the road should be moved. They were told that the government was widening the road to serve people traveling from Ohio to Florida and not just to cater to their community.

Lester's little store had to go. Lester moved to a new location on the road close to his and Betty's home, and this new location was a big mistake.

Other places that have impacted my life are the Nicholson Post Office and the Nicholson Baptist Church. Marilyn and I attended the Nicholson Baptist church from 2001 to 2014. We really enjoyed worshiping our Lord at Nicholson Baptist. Marilyn sang in the church choir and taught a middle-aged couple's class, with me teaching the class when she needed me. Later, she was transferred to teach an older group of ladies, who had lost their husbands. I was moved to an older adult men's class where, at times, I taught this class. Also, we served on many church committees and served at times on the church deacon board. I enjoyed serving as church greeter.

A lot of our church friends and Lester's store friends wanted me to run for the county District 4 Commissioner's Board. This was around 2002. After much encouragement, with my wife agreeing at that past election time, I joined a two-way race on the Republican ticket with Tony Beaty. On the Democrat ticket was Daniel Sailors.

I remember one of my friends, Mr. John Palmer, remarked to me that I should run on the Democrat ticket, that not many people in District 4 voted Republican.

In the end, I was leading by around 90 votes, with only Tony Beaty's home area to report. For some reason, it took a long time for them to report in the election headquarters courthouse. I lost in the end by 64 votes, less than 1% of the total votes, which meant I could ask for a recount. I decided not to contest the final vote. Later, I was told by the court clerk that what held up the precinct where Mr. Beaty lived was that they had to let some people in the that precinct vote in the adjoining one, for some reason. I never understood why.

In 2005, the member of the county Tax Assessors Board resigned from District 4 area. I was asked if I would finish out his term, and I accepted.

To serve on the Board of Tax Assessors, a person must go to a number of classes that are conducted by the

Georgia Department of Revenue. These classes are set up and held at several locations throughout Georgia. I might add that a person cannot get credit for a class by just going to the class because just at the end of the class, a test is given, so it is very wise to spend time after the class each night studying.

After you have taken and passed all tax classes required to serve on a county tax board, you must take one class each year to learn what changes in the tax state laws our state legislators may have made in their legislative session during the year. This class is held each May in Athens at the Continuing Education Center.

As with our National State Teacher Association, there is an Association of Georgia Assessing Officials. Jackson County Tax Board is made up of five members, who meet the second Tuesday at 9:00 a.m. Each member of the board is appointed by the commissioner from his county area. One member, the fifth member, is appointed by the county chairman of the Board of Commissioners. The chairman of our board is voted on by the board members elected each January. I have served on the Jackson County Tax Assessors for the past 13 years, and the newly elected Commissioner, Mr. Marty Seagraves, has just appointed me for another term of three years. I have never missed a tax board meeting in my 13 years on the board. I have been chairman for the past four years.

Truly, I have had many good experiences on the tax board, but I think that where my God wanted me to be working was in county government. The hardest, and yet the best part, is that each May when I go to the Georgia Center, we hold a lot of the training in Tom Mahler Hall, named after the man who was to be my wife Mary Ellen's boss before she passed away. Yes, Mary Ellen, you can look down from heaven and know that the Georgia Center is doing well.

I mentioned that the Nicholson Post Office greatly impacted my life. If you take a look at the picture of girls in Vo Ag, FFA, the young lady seated is Bonnie Corbin. Bonnie married her high school sweetheart, Ted Vaughn, and came to work at our Nicholson Post Office as Mrs. Ted Vaughn. Her husband, Ted, was one of Oconee County's top FFA speakers, and Bonnie was an FFA chapter speaker, charter sweetheart, and also showed heifers and steers with our Oconee County Livestock Show Team.

It was always great to go over the times we shared in Vo Ag class, with me being hers and Ted's teacher and both of them great students. My Vo Ag teacher at Commerce High School once told me it gave him great joy to see his former students doing well in life. The same has been true for me, and I have had that joy many, many times.

Bonnie transferred to the High Shoals Post Office in her home county of Oconee. My wife, Marilyn, and I would stop by and visit her on our way to the state FFA camp. She retired from the Postal Service and joined her husband Ted in a very successful business related to the FFA.

One afternoon, I made a trip to the Nicholson Post Office. There in the front was a new postal lady I had never met. She introduced herself as Vickie Spears. I introduced myself and asked how she was doing. Vickie said, "Not good." She had just lost her husband. Having lost my wife, Mary Ellen, all those memories came rushing back to me. I could really feel the pain that she was feeling, the same pain I felt from losing a good mate. I learned that Vickie's husband, Nolan Spears, was her lifelong sweetheart. They got married right after graduating from Commerce High School, and he passed away in 1997. Like Mary Ellen and me, Nolan and Vickie had two children.

I could not remember seeing Vickie before this time period and learned later that she had been working at the Homer, Georgia, Post Office for about eight years when she returned to the Nicholson Post Office in 2014.

When Vickie returned, she returned as Mrs. Vickie McElroy. She had remarried and her new husband was Ricky McElroy, whom she had married in 2003. Ricky and Vickie were living in the Rogers community where Ricky was raised. This is where they were still living in October 2018.

Renewing my acquaintance when I would make trips to the Nicholson Post Office at times, I would have to wait while she took care of ladies mailing packages. I was really impressed at the way she took care of her customers. One of her customers would bring around a 12-year-old little girl with her and Vickie would let her help with the postal work. I could tell this really meant a lot to the little girl, and when I would come to the post office, many times this little girl would be helping at the post office.

From time to time, Vickie and I had time to talk, and I was amazed that we had so many things in common. It seemed to me that Vickie and I had traveled the same life road. We had both graduated from Commerce High School and had many of the same teachers. We knew a lot of the same people, who had added a lot to both of our lives.

I told Vickie that I was writing my life story and she should be writing her life story. Vickie told me that she had lived a dull life. Much later, I learned why she could not write her life story. Ask me sometimes if you want to know. It is a great reason!

For Marilyn and me, things were not going well in early 2014 at Nicholson Baptist Church. I was serving on the Finance Committee, and the church offering had really fallen off. It seemed that there was going to be a cut in church staff salaries. The Kenneth Slealy family members, who served as Minister of Music and Youth Director, were terminated. This family had done a great job in both church areas.

When talking with Vickie McElroy, she could tell I was having a hard time deciding what Marilyn and I would do. She started to tell me about her church, which was the only church she had ever known as a small child until now. Each week she would bring to me when I came to the post office a copy of the First Baptist Church of Commerce weekly church program. You could tell the church was strong in program structure. Dr. Todd Chandler was director of the church choir. Marilyn was gifted with a great singing voice and I knew she needed to be a part of the Commerce First Baptist Church.

We moved our letter of Christian faith to the Commerce First Baptist Church. Marilyn is singing in the church's great choir. We are in a great Sunday School Bible Study class with great teachers and great fellowship among class members. Marilyn and I can't thank Vickie McElroy enough for her guidance to Commerce First Baptist. Thanks, Vickie.

One of our teachers, Mrs. Becky Perry, has an outstanding knowledge of the Bible, and is also doing a great job as a Sunday School teacher. She closes the class with "His Eye Is on the Sparrow," by Civilla D. Martin, written in 1905[1].

This is a song that always gave me comfort and assurance along life's way. It goes as follows:

His Eye Is on the Sparrow

Why should I feel discouraged

Why should the shadows come

Why should my heart be lonely

And long for heaven and home

When Jesus is my portion?

My constant Friend is He.

His eye is on the sparrow

And I know He watches me.

I sing because I'm happy

I sing because I'm free

For His eye is on the sparrow

And I know He watches me.

"Let not your heart be troubled"

His tender word I hear

---

[1] Public domain

And resting on His goodness

I lose my doubts and fears.

Though by the path He leadeth

But one stop I may see.

His eye is on the sparrow

And I know He watches me.

Whenever I am tempted

Whenever clouds arise

When songs give place to sighing

When hope within me dies

I draw the closer to Him

From care He sets me free.

His eye is on the sparrow

And I know He watches me.

Appendices

Appendix 1: Letters and Documents

Kenneth R. Bridges
1040 White Oak Drive
Athens, GA

Born: 11/28/37, Danielsville, GA

Employment Record:

Position	Employer	City	State	Dates
Teacher of Agriculture	Oconee County Board of Education	Watkinsville	GA	July 1968-Present
Teacher of Agriculture	Towns County Board of Education	Hiawassee	GA	July 1965-July 1968
Teacher of Agriculture	Union County Board of Education	Blairsville	GA	July 1960-July 1965

Professional Education:

Degree	Institution	Year	Major Field
Graduate	Commerce High School	1955	Graduate
BSA	University of Georgia	1960	Agricultural Education
MED	University of Georgia	1972	Agricultural Education

The following are some of the highlights of my years as teacher of Agricultural Education in the school system.

- Received Georgia's Star Teacher award having 10 former students to become teachers of agriculture.

- Five state winning Dairy Product's teams.

- Four state winning and Land Judging teams.

- Trained winning FFA Public Speakers, Forestry teams, Parliamentary teams.

- In 1983, Oconee County FFA chapter's Charles Hillsman was selected as Southern Region Star Farmer of America.

- In 1985, Oconee County FFA exhibited the winning group of 5 heifers at the State 4-H, FFA heifer show.

- As Advisor for Union, Towns, Oconee County FFA chapters, I have had 9 students to serve as State FFA Officers.

- Four District Chapter Achievement winners, one State National Chapter Achievement winner.

- District and State winners in EMC wiring and Georgia Power Electrification contests.

- Four FFA String Band State winners, two FFA Quartet winners.

- Awarded Honorary State Farmer, American Farmer degrees.

Community Service:

- Served as Georgia's youngest Kiwanis Club President, Blairsville, Georgia Club President at age of 22.

- Charter member of Oconee County Lion's Club.

- Consultant & member of Oconee County Young Farmer's Organization.

- Consultant & member of Clarke, Oconee Farm Bureau.

- Consultant, & member of Clarke, Oconee County Pork Producers, Cattlemen Associations.

- Member of Professional Organizations, GATVA, GVA and NATVA.

- Baptist Faith - Presently serving as Deacon of Watkinsville First Baptist Church.

November 23, 1987

Dr. Maynard J. Iverson, Head
Agricultural Education
University of Georgia
Athens, GA 30602

Dear Dr. Iverson:

I am indeed very honored to know that you have nominated me for the prestigious Robert Knowles Memorial Award. This is to let you know that if I am selected for this honor that I will certainly be willing to attend the annual GATE Conference on January 21-22 at the Macon Hilton. Thank you for your consideration.

Yours truly,

Kenneth R. Bridges

Kenneth R. Bridges
Teacher of Agriculture
Oconee County High School
Watkinsville, GA 30677

NCCAT

at WESTERN CAROLINA UNIVERSITY
Cullowhee, North Carolina 28723
Telephone (704) 227-7370

November 8, 1988

Mr. Kenneth Bridges
Oconee County High School
Hog Mountain Road
Watkinsville, GA 30677

Dear Mr. Bridges:

On behalf of my colleagues in the Georgia Association of Teacher
Educators, I am pleased to notify you that you have been selected
as the 1988-89 recipient of the Association's Robert Knowles
Memorial Award for Outstanding Supervising Teacher of the Year.
The fact that the competition was stiff should make you doubly
proud of your achievements as a student, a classroom teacher, and
most notably, as a supervising teacher.

Joining me on the selection committee were Ms. Jewell Biggs
(Fulton County Schools), Ms. Beth McKinnon (Mercer University
Atlanta), and Dr. May Newby (Mercer University Atlanta). All
four of us were impressed by the obvious high regard in which you
are held by the faculty at The University of Georgia as well as
your principal and former student teachers.

The Association will hold its annual meeting this coming Wednesday, Thursday, and Friday, November 9-11 at the Athens Holiday
Inn. A copy of the program is enclosed and we hope that you can
join us. In any event, though, we look forward to your being
with us for the Thursday evening banquet at 7:00 when the Knowles
Award will be presented to you.

Once again, let me say congratulations and thank you for the very
considerably time, energy, and competence you have provided for
the improvement of education in the state of Georgia.

Sincerely yours,

Jerome D. Franson

Jerome D. Franson
Chairman, Knowles Award Committee
Professor (on leave), Georgia College
NCCAT Fellow

JDF/nne
Enclosure
pc: Dr. Maynard J. Iverson
     Mr. Tony Dukes

BOARD OF TRUSTEES:
J. Carlyle Sitterson, chairperson
John A. Tate, Jr., vice chairperson

William Baggett
Jerry L. Cole
George Collins

Myron L. Coulter
Hubert A. Eaton, Sr.
Alice J. Garrett

Sarah E. Himan
Pamela Mayer
Charles C. McConnell, Jr.

A. Craig Phillips
H. F. Robinson
C. Dixon Spangler

Elise Wilson
BOARD LIAISON: Donald J. Stedman
DIRECTOR R. Bruce McPherson

An Affirmative Action/Equal Opportunity Employer

KENNETH BRIDGES

149

Department of Agricultural Education

629 Aderhold Hall
The University of Georgia
Athens, Georgia 30602
(404) 542-1204

November 24, 1987

To Whom It May Concern:

I have known Mr. Kenneth Bridges for the past 30 years and I have worked with him while I served as a staff member in the Department of Agricultural Education for the past 15 years. During these years I have worked with Mr. Bridges while he served as a supervising teacher of our students on several occasions.

Mr. Bridges has always had a very cooperative attitude as far as working with us here at the University is concerned. If the occasion arose when we had a student who needed special attention as a student teacher, we would probably place him/her with Mr. Bridges at Oconee County High School. He always did an excellent job of supervising student teachers. He always set an example by demonstrating the characteristics of a master teacher.

On several occasions we have had international students who did not want to do student teaching, and who could not because of difficulty with the English language. We would request that Mr. Bridges permit these students to do an internship of primarily observation with him. He always was very cooperative in working with these students.

As the instructor of the curriculum planning course in Agricultural Education, I have carried the class to Oconee County High School to discuss with Mr. Bridges the job of a teacher of vocational agriculture. Although Mr. Bridges had a class of his own at the time, he always found a way to talk to my students.

Even though Mr. Bridges had several years of experience working with student teachers, he registered for the internship in supervising student teachers winter quarter, 1987. He was not using the course toward a degree. He just wanted to be fully certified as a supervising teacher.

Mr. Bridges is recognized state wide as one of the best teachers of vocational agriculture in Georgia. He is also, in my opinion, one of the best supervising teachers in the state.

Sincerely,

Thomas C. Weaver, Public Service Assoc.
Agricultural Education

Georgia Department of Education
Office of Instructional Programs
603 Driftmier Engineering Center
Athens, Georgia 30602

Werner Rogers
State Superintendent of Schools

December 11, 1987

Peyton Williams Jr.
Associate State Superintendent

William P. Johnson
Assistant State Superintendent
General and Vocational Instruction

Don Hogan
Assistant State Superintendent
Special Instructional Programs

Dr. Maynard J. Iverson, Head
Agricultural Education
629 Aderhold Hall, UGA
Athens, Georgia 30602

Dear Dr. Iverson:

It is with a great deal of pride and pleasure that I recommend Mr. Kenneth Bridges for the prestigious Robert Knowles Memorial Award for Outstanding Supervising Teacher of the Year. His achievements and his impact on students of vocational agriculture are enormous, and his credentials as a professional educator are of the highest caliber.

The results of his twenty-seven years teaching experience as a high school vocational agriculture teacher can be felt throughout Georgia's educational and agribusiness sectors. Mr. Bridges also serves as advisor to the Oconee County Chapter Future Farmers of America and is highly recognized for his leadership training ability as exemplified by their outstanding accomplishments in district, state, and national contests. The chapter has been recognized as a Gold Emblem Chapter several times and as a State Chapter Achievement winner.

Mr. Bridges has provided an opportunity for University of Georgia students majoring in Agricultural Education to visit as a group or individually to observe classroom teaching strategy. He is untiring in his efforts to assist apprentice teachers in obtaining the most out of their apprenticeship program.

Mr. Bridges is an active member of many local, state, and national professional teacher organizations. He has served as a District III Director of the Georgia Vocational Agriculture Teachers Association and has been recognized for his outstanding achievements as a classroom teacher.

I count it an honor to have been given the opportunity to recommend Mr. Kenneth Bridges for this award. He certainly exemplifies those qualities that make him very deserving of this recognition.

Sincerely,

D. G. Farmer
Assistant State Supervisor
Agricultural Education

Oconee County High School

P. O. Box 534
WATKINSVILLE, GEORGIA 30677

December 2, 1987

To Whom It May Concern:

It is a pleasure for me to recommend Mr. Kenneth Bridges to you for your consideration. I have known Kenneth for approximately eight (8) years. Kenneth is currently one of two agriculture teachers at OCHS and has served in this position for 20 years.

Kenneth Bridges is a dedicated agriculture teacher. He spends an enormous amount of time working with his students, both teaching and supervising at school and away from school. One has only to look in his classroom to see all of the awards and trophies that his students have won under his direction and supervision. Kenneth is an energetic individual, willing to work long hours in preparing his students for upcoming shows, contests, and events. He has also had numerous opportunities to supervise college student teachers and field experience students. You can be sure that these student teachers will benefit from the apprenticeship with Kenneth.

Kenneth is an asset to the teaching profession and we are very fortunate and happy to have him on the staff at OCHS.

Sincerely,

Tony Dukes
Principal

Georgia Electrification Council, Inc.
Driftmier Engineering Center
Athens, Georgia 30602
404 542-3293

H. Cecil Beggs
Executive Director

December 11, 1987

Maynard J. Iverson
Department of Agricultural Education
629 Aderhold Hall
The University of Georgia
Athens, GA 30602

Dear Maynard:

As a co-member of the Vocational Agricultural family, I have worked with Mr. Kenneth Bridges for the past 20 years and fully appreciate his contribution in the development of young Vo-Ag teachers in Georgia. It is, therefore, an honor for me to recommend Mr. Bridges for the Robert Knowles Memorial Award for the 1988 Outstanding Supervising Teacher of the Year.

Mr. Bridges has the ability to uniquely combine hard work, practical applications and sound vocational philosophy with a warm and helpful personality. His "winning ways" and dedication to helping people "do better" certainly qualify him for this award.

One of Mr. Bridges distinguishing characteristics is "he is always there." If you needed a school to visit for observation—he was always willing to accommodate. If you needed a supervising center for special students—he was always available. If you needed a cheerleader for vocational agriculture—he was always ready. Yes, Mr. Bridges has made his contribution to our program and to the many students who have sought his advise and guidance as they begin their teaching careers. He is well deserving of this prestigious award.

Thank you for considering Mr. Bridges' application.

Sincerely,

Cecil

H. Cecil Beggs
Executive Director

HCB:jh

Georgia Department of Education
Office of Instructional Programs
603 Driftmier Engineering Center
Athens, Georgia 30602

Werner Rogers
State Superintendent of Schools

December 7, 1987

Peyton Williams Jr.
Associate State Superintendent

William P. Johnson
Assistant State Superintendent
General and Vocational Instruction

Don Hogan
Assistant State Superintendent
Special Instructional Programs

Dr. Maynard J. Iverson, Head
Agricultural Education
629 Aderhold Hall, UGA
Athens, Georgia 30602

Dear Dr. Iverson:

With a great deal of pleasure I would certainly recommend Mr. Kenneth Bridges for the
Robert Knowles Memorial Award for Outstanding Supervising Teacher of the Year, 1988.
I have known Mr. Bridges for some years, but have specifically observed his outstanding skills as a teacher of vocational agriculture since 1968 which was the year I
entered the teaching profession. Through the years Mr. Bridges has been outstanding
in many areas, but his record in livestock production is one of excellence. He has
always participated in all of the junior livestock shows in Georgia such as the steer,
heifer, market hog, and purebred swine shows. Not only has he participated, but his
FFA students have won district and state awards too numerous to mention in this letter.
Mr. Bridges has also arranged financial assistance, through a local bank, for many of
his students who needed financial help in their supervised occupational program. This
assistance has helped many students actually get started in the cattle business and
other agricultural enterprises.

One specific aspect of his career is that he has encouraged students to use Shorthorn
breeding stock for their project programs. Because other breeds of cattle are so preva-
lent in his county, he encouraged them to select a breed, such as Shorthorn cattle,
that offered a greater marketing advantage. Today, Georgia's finest purebred Shorthorn
cattle graze the pastures of Oconee County which is due entirely to the foresight of
Mr. Bridges. All of these herds are owned by his former students who had a Shorthorn
heifer as their project program in high school.

Another distinct quality of Mr. Bridges' career has been his dedication to having a
quality adult education program in his community. Not only does he provide adult classes
in livestock production, but also in other areas, such as agricultural mechanics. Mr.
Bridges also gives the student teachers who he is supervising at the time, definite
responsibilities in organizing and conducting the adult classes. He always stresses
the importance of public relations through his adult program.

In summary, I believe Mr. Bridges motto might be "Excellence in Agricultural Education
and Service to my Fellow Man". Not only has he emphasized excellence in the classroom,
but also his service to his community, students, and his school is unequalled.

Sincerely,

Billy Moss
Area Livestock Teacher
Agricultural Education

COOPERATIVE EXTENSION SERVICE

THE UNIVERSITY OF GEORGIA COLLEGE OF AGRICULTURE

201 S. Beachview Drive
Jekyll Island, GA 31520
December 1, 1987

Dr. M.J. Iverson
Dept. of Ag. Education
629 Adernold Hall
The University of Georgia
Athens, GA 30602

Dear Dr. Iverson,

I am delighted to hear that you are nominating Mr. Kenneth
Bridges for the prestigous Robert Knowles Memorial Award.
You would be hard pressed to find a more deserving person.

Mr. Bridges worked closely with me throughout my graduate
studies in agricultural education. As my supervising
teacher, he was quite effective in helping me to learn how
to be most effective in my teaching efforts. His genuine
love for teaching shows in everything he does. This ever-
present attitude brings the most positive responses from
students and apprentices.

One could not begin to list the attributes of Kenneth
Bridges. It is against his program and record that all
others in Georgia are judged.

Thank you for you time in consideration of Mr. Kenneth
Bridges for the Robert Knowles Award. I am,

Sincerely yours,

C. Alan Sikes
Education Program Specialist
Jekyll Island, Georgia

Sandhills Community College

2200 AIRPORT ROAD
PINEHURST, NORTH CAROLINA 28374
PHONE: 919-692-6185

December 9, 1987

Department of Agricultural Education
629 Aderhold Hall
University of Georgia
Athens, Georgia   30602

To Whom It May Concern:

I was most pleased to learn that Mr. Kenneth Bridges is being nominated
for the Robert Knowles Memorial Award. I can think of no one who should
be recognized for his/her work with Apprentice Teachers more than he.

Since Apprentice Teaching under Mr. Bridges during the Fall of 1985, I
have come to know him better as a person and peer. Certainly my appreciation for his guidance during that phase of my training is much greater
now. The things that stand out the most in my mind are: his classroom
management skills, his command of technical subject matter, his devotion
to his job, and his keen interest in his students' development.

Mr. Bridges has always been keenly aware of the educational needs of the
agricultural sector of his area, as evidenced by the classes he teaches,
both in-school and for adults after school. He manages those classes
and lab settings to maintain student interest and maximize content. He
stays abreast of technical development in his subject areas both by continuing his education and remaining active in the agricultural industry.
He gives unselfishly of his time, far beyond what is expected or remuner-
ated. He strives to insure that each student participates actively in
the Future Farmers of America, that the FFA Chapter participates qualita-
tively in every activity, and that each student has a quality Supervised
Occupational Experience Program. One look at the many awards the students
have won over the years is quick testimony to his success.

Furthermore, I find his interpersonal traits to be second to none. While
striving toward his own and his students' perfection, he does not sacri-
fice patience and consideration for others. His attention to detail while
maintaining a hectic pace has been inspiring to me. In short, I sincerely hope he will be awarded this honor.

Respectfully submitted,

Daniel Oglesby
MEd-AgEd, 1987

Oconee County High School

P. O. Box 534
WATKINSVILLE, GEORGIA 30677

December 1, 1987

To Whom It May Concern:

This letter is in reference to the nomination of Mr. Kenneth R.
Bridges for the Robert Knowles Memorial Award for Outstanding
Supervising Teacher of the year. It has been my pleasure to have been
associated with Mr. Bridges since 1972 when, as an aspiring agriculture
teacher, I visited Oconee County High and observed Mr. Bridges' class-
room techniques. I was later fortunate to work side-by-side with
Kenneth for three years as a fellow vocational agriculture teacher at
Oconee County High School.

In those years, 1975-78, I developed a deep appreciation for the
unique teaching style Kenneth had. He proved to be the type of teacher
that is loved by students, not for his position, but for his interest
in them as individuals. There is no doubt in my mind that Kenneth has
been the catalyst that prompted many former students to get interested
in school (especially through FFA activities) and stay in school.

Kenneth has a strong interest in the livestock curriculum of our
vocational agriculture program. This interest is contagious among the
students and is reflected in the years of success Oconee County High
School FFA has enjoyed in livestock exhibits and competition. Many
fellow vocational agriculture instructors are aware of the challenge
of going up against students and livestock that Mr. Bridges has had a
hand in preparing for show.

Kenneth has a long history of unparalleled success in most competitive events in the FFA organization. His prowess in livestock,
soil judging, and forestry competitive events is recognized throughout
the state. The walls of his classroom and office are lined with plaques
and trophies won by students over the years. In 1983, Charles Hillsman,
a former Oconee County High School vocational agriculture student was
recognized as the Star Farmer from the Southern Region. Kenneth was
quite instrumental in providing the direction Charles needed for reaching
this goal.

In 1981, Oconee County High School became a "comprehensive" high
school and I assumed the role as vocational supervisor. Although our
working relationship has changed, Kenneth continues to work hard for the
vocational agriculture program. He has been an enthusiastic supporter
of vocational education throughout our school, community and state.

We have had quite a number of students serve quarterly internships
and student teaching at Oconee County High School with Kenneth over the

years. I don't know the exact number, but would guess that probably more students enrolled in Agricultural Education have visited our school and/or served an internship period here than at any other school in the state. Kenneth has also worked with quite a number of foreign agriculture students over the years. Each spring, the UGA Agriculture Education Department has brought a class of seniors out to visit Kenneth and ask questions about teaching vocational agriculture. Also, during the summer months, Kenneth has hosted a number of state vocational agriculture in-service workshops for teachers.

The histroy of involvement in preparing young men and women to teach vocational agriculture is a testament to the value of his training input. You don't continue to utilize people who have nothing positive to offer.

Kenneth is a strong believer in the saying "you learn by doing." He incorporates hands-on activities and field trips into all of his teaching ventures. Students remember these things for years.

He works hard, he's dedicated to vocational agriculture as a program and its career opportunities, and he's genuinely concerned with serving those who are hungry for knowledge. He has served this program, school, and community well, but, has served the youth of our school even more. He deserves recognition for his committment and dedication. I strongly support his nomination for this award.

Sincerely,

Dennis A. Clarke

Dennis A. Clarke, Ed. D.
Vocational Supervisor

DAC:ld

142 Firewood St.
Athens, GA   30605
(404) 354-8118
June 7, 1987

Mr. Kenneth Bridges
2323 Macon Highway
Athens, GA   30606

Dear Mr. Bridges:

Just a note to let you know I took a position as Physical Plant Manager with Sandhills Community College in Pinehurst, NC. It is a very good job, with much better pay than I could get as a starting teacher anywhere in Georgia or NC, and has great opportunity.

I especially want to thank you for your generous letters of recommendation. I am sure that it had a lot to do with the many job offers I received, especially to teach, both in NC and Georgia, as well as the one I finally took.

I would like to somehow return the favor in kind. If you ever figure out some way that I can do anything for you, please let me know. And certainly, if you and Mrs. Bridges are ever up in our new neck-of-the-woods, please be sure to look us up.

Sincerely,

Daniel Oglesby

Daniel Oglesby

April 25, 1980

Mr. and Mrs. Dan M. Barrett
650 LaVista Road
Athens, Georgia 30606

Mr. Kenneth Bridges
Oconee County High School
Vocational Agriculture Department
P. O. Box 534
Watkinsville, Georgia 30677

Dear Kenneth:

In this "take for granted" world, too often we never take
the opportunity to recognize outstanding achievement, but last
night Brenda and I had the pleasure of seeing a great number
of fine young people recognized for their many positive
endeavors. It became very apparent that the success enjoyed
by these young people was the direct result of the leadership you have so generously provided.

Kenneth, I should think that you would feel a real sense
of accomplishment in being so instrumental in the development
of our most valuable resource -- our youth. Oconee County
and the kids will benefit for years to come from your efforts.
For those efforts, we thank you.

Best of luck and continued success for you and yours.

Sincerely,

Dan and Brenda Barrett

DMB/mcj

Closing Remarks – Young Farmer's Program
David Mooney

HONORING KENNETH ROGERS BRIDGES
Opening Remarks – Tim Brooks

KENNETH'S FAMILY
Comments by Thomas Bridges, Brother

SCHOOL DAYS FOR KENNETH
Roy E. Powell, High School Teacher

AGRICULTURE TEACHER
Fellow Ag. Teacher/Student Teacher Supervisor
Dr. Thomas Weaver

FORMER STUDENT COMMENTS
Scott Jordan, State FFA Officer

FORMER STUDENT/STATE STAFF RELATIONSHIPS
Gary Farmer

ADMINISTRATION/SUPERVISION OF KENNETH
James R. Gurley, Principal

JACKSON COUNTY YOUNG FARMER PROGRAM
SPECIAL PRESENTATIONS
Tim Brooks

CLOSING REMARKS
Kenneth Rogers Bridges

Please sign card for Kenneth on table near
bulletin board; also complete form for scrapbook
if you have not already done so.

National Kennel Club, Inc.®

Champion Dogs, Champion Owners, Champion Service.

An All-Breed Registry
Since 1964
Reg. U.S. Patent Office

American Rabbit Hound Association

Licensed Kennel

This certifies that BRIDGES RABBITMASTER HOUNDS is licensed by the National Kennel Club, Inc. and promises to uphold the high standards set forth by the National Kennel Club, Inc. and this kennel.

BRIDGES RABBITMASTER HOUNDS

KENNETH & MAILYN BRIDGES, OWNER(S)

Valid 8/2/2007 through 8/2/2008

Jackson
County
Young
Farmers

Banquet
Tuesday, May 12, 1992
7:30 p.m.
J.C.C.H.S. Cafeteria

The Jackson County Young Farmers welcome you to our banquet.

Meal	Compliments of Mr. Kenny Gee and Jackson County Farm Bureau
Invocation	Kenneth Bridges Young Farmer Advisor
Welcome	Recognition special guest Dwight Cooper, President
Greeting	Georgia State Young Farmer's Association Introduction-Greg Pittman, Treasurer
Entertainment	Band Introduction-Tim Brooks, Vice President
Farm Family Award	Farm Credit Services Introduction-Brant McMullan, Reporter
Guest speaker	Introduction-Steve Childs, Secretary
Closing remarks	David Mooney, Sentinel

RESUME

Mary Ellen Davis Bridges - Phone 404-757-2465   June 1978
Born in Miami, Dade County, Florida, on January 25, 1940

EDUCATION:

A. A.   Graduated from Young Harris College, Young Harris, Georgia, in
          March 1963.

          Studies included liberal arts - two year (A.A.) degree and all
business courses, clerical and secretarial; received two-year clerical and
secretarial certificate. Last two courses taken during two quarters I was
employed full time in dean's office. Active in church, high school, and
community activities during college enrollment.

High   Graduated from Buford High School, Buford, Georgia, in June 1958.
School   Studies included business courses and general curriculum. Honors in
          scholastic achievement and shorthand (8/56 with 93.6 average).
          Activities: Beta Club, Tri-Hi Y, FHA Club, Annual Staff, District
Meet representative - shorthand.

WORK EXPERIENCE: 10 years 3 months

March 8, 1976   UNIVERSITY OF GEORGIA
     to   Secretary (IV) to Associate Director for Instruction,
Present   Georgia Center for Continuing Education. This is an
                       executive secretarial position. It is the senior
                       secretarial position in a department consisting of
68 professional staff members and 46 clerical personnel. It is interrelated with
all aspects of the Georgia Center including the other two major departments of
Managerial Services and Communications Services and maintains complex relationships
with departments, schools, and colleges throughout the campus.

     Specifically, the duties of the position include normal secretarial services,
editing correspondence and manuscripts, maintaining day-to-day operational faculty
extra compensation records, overall supervision of the Center's data processing
records and staff, and general office management. It requires the development and
maintenance of effective working relationships with the offices of the University's
central administration and with the offices of the University's academic deans.
It also involves continuous contact and interface with both leaders and the general
citizenry of Athens and the surrounding areas.

     During my tenure in this position, I have reorganized the files and implemented
a sophisticated and highly effective recordkeeping system for the office.

Experience: Typewriter, shorthand, telephone, 10-key calculator, IBM portable
dictaphone transcriber, Xerox and IBM copiers.

Currently employed - June 1978.

July 1, 1975   UNIVERSITY OF GEORGIA
    to   Secretary (III) to Director of Business Services
March 6, 1976   Division, Manager of Auxiliary and Administrative
                    Services, Business Manager, and Information Specialist.
                    This was a one-secretary office.

Major responsibilities included record management; dictaphone transcription; distribution of mail; making travel arrangements, keeping appointment schedules, processing travel expense statements; telephone, public relations; typing (legal contracts, all business forms including personnel, camera-ready newsletters, progress reports, budget amendments, journal vouchers, payroll vouchers, and general correspondence); reconcilment of operating expense accounts for four departments; prepare, check, and compile progress reports for division; distributing status reports for division. Totally responsible for secretarial duties required for the smooth operation of the manager of Auxiliary and Administrative Services who was responsible for 10 units and the Director of Busines Services Division as related to the Auxiliary and Administrative Services Department as well as to Materials Management Department with five units. Also provided total secretarial support for Business Manager who was responsible for the fiscal affairs and operations for the division. Provided secretarial support for Information Specialist which included news articles, newsletters, letters, orders, and general correspondence. Developed and set up first comprehensive filing system for all Business Services Division recordkeeping.

Experience: Telephone, typewriter, IBM dictaphone transcriber, 10-key calculator, Xerox copier, citizens band radio, and light shorthand.

Transferred from the Secretary III position to Secretary IV position.

December 30, 1974   UNIVERSITY OF GEORGIA
    to   Secretary (I) in Loan Funds Department to two loan
June 30, 1975   collection officers whose principle responsibilities were
                    collecting delinquent accounts. My main responsibilities
                    were daily correspondence, monthly report of delinquent
accounts and progress reports, form letters, notices, and excessive shorthand dictation, light phone use, Xerox copier, and filing. Assisted with reconcilment of loan accounts each month.

Experience: Typewriter, shorthand, 10-key calculator, telephone.

Transferred from this Secretary I position to Secretary III position.

GOALS:

I enjoy working with people, being responsible and accountable for interaction with others, learning new concepts and skills to broaden my sphere of activity in the business field. At the same time, I take great pride in my work, try especially hard to do a creditable job whether the task is particularly challenging or as minimal as filing. Conscientiousness, dependability, cooperation, and cheerfulness rank high among my personal standards. I find it easy to maintain a flexible schedule to meet the needs of my immediate supervisor. I enjoy figures (accounting), do not mind repetition, but do not hesitate to take on a new assignment.

I enjoy quiet country living with my family and friends and relate well with all social levels. I find it quite satisfying to come into the business setting and interact with associates performing in a professional atmosphere. The feelings of accomplishment, success, and stability are gratifying.

PERSONAL DATA:

Address:	Route 4, Box 74-A, Commerce, Georgia 30529
Married to:	Kenneth Rogers Bridges on March 27, 1959
Children:	Son - Starling - Age 11 years Daughter - Shannon - Age 9 years
Interests:	Enjoy participating in swimming, jogging, hiking, yoga; spectator for basketball and football.

I have a keen interest in nutrition, health, and sewing clothes for my family. I enjoy cooking, machine embroidery, growing house plants, gardening, knitting and crocheting. My relaxing activities include reading, television, instrumental and country music.

Outside
Interests: Berea Baptist Church, Commerce, Georgia - Member and teacher of Sunday School.

Future Farmers of America-Oconee County Chapter - Training public speaking participants; write and type newspaper articles.

Family Farm - actively involved in management of total operation, selection and care of registered beef cattle on the farm and preparation of show calves for shows.

Children's activities - close involvement at school as grademother, in PTA; at home with children in reading, handicrafts, farm work; and in a variety of activities for the children such as clogging, horseback riding, camping, roller skating, etc.

Collector of photographs, amateur movie camera operator.

August 26, 1968   UNIVERSITY OF GEORGIA
to   Secretary of Mental Health Division, University Health
April 30, 1969   Services. Coordinated initial stages of Mental Health
                         Division consisting of 12 to 15 doctors; set up forms,
                         schedules, and letters for 12 to 15 mental health
psychiatrists, psychologists, and counselors; received routine mental health
clients as well as emergency mental patients; assisted with appointment scheduling.
Served as supervisor in Medical Records transcription section; typed all mental
health case notes from dictaphone and maintained confidentiality of
cases. Supervised three girls in transcription of physical health case notes
and filing for front reception desk.

Experience: Typewriter, telephone, and Nymatic Dictaphone System.

Terminated due to pregnancy.

September 15, 1962   YOUNG HARRIS COLLEGE
to   Secretary to Dean of Students and Director of Admissions
September 30, 1966   and supervised two work study students. This office was
                         the hub of student activities on campus and the point of
                         contact for prospective students and their parents.
Duties included public relations, typing, shorthand, telephone, traffic, student
activities, disciplinary actions, housing, admissions, recruitment for enrollment,
analysis and selection of recipients for financial aid and candidates for admission.
Activities included work with currently enrolled students, prospective students,
parents, faculty, staff and dormitory personnel.

Experience: Typewriter, shorthand, telephone.

Terminated due to pregnancy.

July 16, 1958   SEARS, ROEBUCK AND COMPANY
to   Bookkeeper in Auditing Department, 675 Ponce de Leon
September 16, 1960   Avenue, N.E., Atlanta, for two controlling accounts -
                         employee house sales and transfer of sales and accounts
                         from one Sears store to another. Constant work with
figures, balancing reports, journal entries, telephone, charge-out reports,
reconciliation.

Experience: 10-key calculator, telephone.

Terminated to go with husband.

Appendix 2: Photos

Buddy and Buster

buster's 1st. christmas

The Oconee High School FFA Chapter placed first in the recent forestry field day activities at Whitehall. They will compete in the State finals on May 10 at the Veterans State Park near Cordele. Front row, L-R, are Jeff Dawson, Herman Smith, Greg Peck, Chistina Clement, John Van Gotum, Rodney Jordan and Bobby Hale. Back row, L-R, are Star Bridges, David Butler, Fran Whitehead, Donald Hansford and Kenneth Bridges, advisor.

Appendix 3: Articles

Buckeye, Hostess, and the Rabbit Master Hounds
By Kenneth R. Bridges

Rabbit hunting has always been a burning passion for me. My dad introduced it to me as a small boy growing up in Northeast Georgia in the 1940s and 50s. During this time we hunted for the meat and things were really different than today. There were lots of Cotton Tails and Cane Cutters, also called Buck Rabbits, that lived along large streams or anywhere undrained swamps occurred. There were no deer until they were reintroduced into Northeast Georgia by the Department of Natural Resources in the early 1960s.

It was a thrill for me helping my dad track down a rabbit in the snow. As a teenager in the 50s, plowing a mule, hoeing and picking cotton, it was a thrill to take time out to hear our mixed hounds really drive a rabbit. Our rabbit hounds consisted of: Bulldog/Red Bone, Terrier/Beagle cross and even Black and Tan/German Shepherd cross. You would be surprised how well some of our mixed dogs could run a rabbit when they had someone who really took the time to train them. During this period of time in my life, fox hunting was very popular throughout the Southeast. There were no deer, not many paved highways, and lots of gray and red foxes. Our next door neighbor, Mr. Hubert Mealor, kept fox hounds, mostly July/Walker hounds. Mr. Mealor also had five strange type hounds that he called Wire-haired hounds.

One Sunday morning after getting ready for church, I heard a pack of hounds in full cry coming down a creek below our house. Wanting to get a closer look at the action I ran down the road just in time to see Mr. Mealor with a rock in hand to throw at a fox crossing the road. Very close behind the fox was Mr. Mealor's wire-haired hounds. He explained to me that the hounds had been running this fox for about five years. He later told me that they caught him half an hour after I saw the fox cross the road. Mr. Mealor is running fox in heaven now, and his son, Jerry, could not give me any information on his wire-haired hounds. I remember being in bed lots of nights and a pack of fox hounds would bring a fox by our place in full cry. I would thrill to great "hound" music again. The most beautiful voice I have ever heard on a hound was a July that took up at our home after being lost in a fox race. The hound stayed with us and we ran rabbits with him for two weeks. He had a voice like a bugle at its best.

My first introduction to purebred Beagles was after becoming a Teacher of Agriculture at Blairsville, GA in 1960. A young drugstore owner, Mr. Charles Hill, was purchasing some fine gundog type beagles from a friend, Mr. Bill Watts of Akron, OH. Charles said his time was very limited, and he asked me to run his beagles on his farm for him. In his kennel there was a male named Buckeye, who was a 15" saddleback with an outstanding voice and a far better than average nose. About this time, I had traded a Redbone coon hound for a Bluetick Beagle female, pedigree unknown. I bred my beagle to Buckeye with the results being six pups. At five weeks of age, one pup died leaving me with three males and three females. Each Wednesday after school, and on Saturdays this pack of five was loaded into the trunk of my 1956 Ford convertible for training, gundog style. An article in one of my Rabbit Hunter magazines explained how important it is to match dogs of same age and speed. I have every copy of the Rabbit Hunter magazine from the first copy printed in September 1, 1986. My address was printed by longhand on the front cover. Needless to say, I really enjoy this magazine and, and really enjoy the present issues with the increased rabbit hunting stories and special features.

Now back to my five beagles that I kept for eight years before losing two. This pack either put a rabbit in a hole or caught every rabbit they jumped. If my shotgun didn't score, these hounds didn't ever break the skin on a rabbit bringing them to me, carrying the rabbit by the back of the neck. All five of these beagles would bring a caught rabbit to me.

Teaching agriculture for eight years in the North Georgia Mountains at Blairsville and Hiawasee (1960-68), I had many a great race in the long mountain corn bottoms and up the side of deep mountains. However, I think my greatest rabbit race with these five came one Sunday morning on a creek called Sandy Creek here in Commerce GA where I now live. This creek had lots of swamp ponds ad lots of big buck swamp rabbits. Buck Rabbits like to swim through the ponds of water to elude your hounds. On this crisp December morning, my five hounds really locked onto a buck rabbit who had them down the creek through ponds out of my hearing and back twice. Realizing he could not lose the dogs on the creek bottom, he left the swamp for a large oak grove. I shot him on his way back, just a very short distances ahead of the dogs. The only part about his rabbit race was I was the only one enjoying it. I have wished many times I had a recording of this race so I could listen to it often.

Buckeye is now known in the Blairsville Georgia area as the "Million Dollar Beagle." Mr. Charles Hill tells me that he went to Lake Nottley, a lake lot auction where he bought ten lots. Charles Hill was so impressed with Buckeye's ability that he offered to trade Mr. Bill Watts the ten lakeside lots for Buckeye. Mr. Watts accepted this offer. Mr. Watts kept these lots, and as the North Georgia mountains developed, he recently sold them for over one million dollars. Never can tell what a good hound might be worth.

I kept my pack of five beagles in the same pen. I would take the two females by my vet's twice a year for a shot to keep them from coming into heat. It worked well, and when I bred the two females around five years, the results were two nice litters of pups. My vet now tells me they were using a human hormone and they are not allowed to use this produce at present, something about a possible lawsuit.

Over the past thirty years I have linebred my beagle strain without crosses occasionally to a beagle male that met my requirement for a top-notch rabbit hound. As a teacher of agriculture working with students on swine and cattle breeding projects, I noticed we produced our best animals when we linebred family lines. I have maintained since 1966 a registered Polled Shorthorn herd. Line breeding families of good cattle produces top quality cattle.

With the above induction of my hunting/breeding experience, let me now introduce you to my Rabbit Master Hounds. The Rabbit Master hound is composed of ½ Beagle, ¼ English Bassett, and ¼ Vendeen Griffon Petite French Bassett. I was introduced to the wooly French Bassett when Mr. Ron Swanson brought their Byfield Bassett formal hunting pack to my farm for training. In this pack was a French Bassett that hunted harder for a rabbit than any dog I have ever seen in 50+ years of running rabbit dogs. I mentioned to Mrs. Pat Swanson I would like to cross the French Bassett with a good Beagle. About a year later, the Swansons delivered to me a one half French Basset, and one half English Bassett female. This little female looks like a full Vendeen Griffon Petite French Bassett. This pup, named Hostess, has developed into the best rabbit hound I have ever known.

Being on the fuzzy side, an avid rabbit hunting buddy of mine stated that a hairy dog would not make a good hunting dog. After a time in the field with Hostess, I got great pleasure in seeing him become a great admirer of her. When my hunting buddy goes hunting with me he wants to make sure Hostess is in my pack. To me, one of the most frustrating things in rabbit hunting is not being able to jump a rabbit. No rabbit—No chase. I have had many a hunter tell me that he had a great rabbit running pack, but he needed a jump dog badly. A good example: I was busy working on pasture fence one day when Mr. Walter Embrick and Mr. John Wood showed up with a pack of eight beagles. After an hour hunt, no rabbit had been jumped. These two men pleaded with me to go get my Bassett and let her start them a rabbit. When Hostess was brought to the hunting area, within ten minutes a rabbit was jumped. Catching Hostess up, I took her to her pen and continued my fence work. My friends enjoyed a good rabbit hunt and they were very pleased Hostess came their way.

Another time in the field, Hostess had jumped and was really pushing a rabbit across fields and hedge rows and our Beagle pack was having a hard time completing with the hard driving French Bassett. I told Mr. Walt Embrick the Bassett was running the rabbit like a good rabbit dog runs a rabbit and those Beagles need to step it up a notch.

I have two of what I believe to be great rabbit running male Beagles. They are line bred from the pack I mentioned earlier. When breeding these two males to Hostess, two fine litters of five each were born. There were four slick haired, one wooly haired in each litter. I call them my Rabbit Master Hounds. With ½ French Basset, I have found the answer to finding the rabbit. With ¼ English Bassett, a good nose a great voice, and with ½ Beagle that I think blends the qualities of a great rabbit hound together.

My plans are to breed these dogs and enjoy my love that I found early as a boy—siting on a hill and listening to the thrill of a great pack pushing a rabbit hard, hound music at its best. You can rest assured my pack will be made up of the Rabbit Master Hounds.

--published February 2002 in *The Fox & Coyote Hunter*

Rabbitmaster Hounds and the Lowly Earthworms
By Kenneth R. Bridges

Summer has come to Georgia bringing the wettest conditions (winter or summer) in over 50 years. The weather has been a blessing to people in the cattle business suffering through the summer of 2002 with only three inches of rain.

My kennel presently consists of seven Rabbitmaster hounds, five trained hounds and two started pups. When planning my kennel, I read many articles dealing with the best type of kennel for hunting dogs. With past experiences of free running dogs during the 40s, 50s, and 60s to dirt pens in the 70s and 80s, I came to believe there must be a better way to kennel a good pack of Rabbitmaster hounds. After much research I decided to build a 40' long, 10' wide sloping 4' section concrete pen. In the corner of each pen I built of cyclone fence wire, I hung one 50 gallon plastic drum. The drum makes adequate shelter for my Rabbitmaster hounds as we have relatively mild Georgia winters.

The kennel was built under oak trees providing excellent shade during our hot summers and wind breaks for winter located about 100 yards from my house, and 50 yards from my horse and cattle barn. It is easy to provide a water hose with good water pressure to wash the sloped pens twice a day. I was very pleased with my kennel arrangements for about two years, then a problem began to occur. With leaves falling from my oak trees mixing with the elimination of body waste from my Rabbitmaster hounds I began to get a build up of organic matter at the back of the pens. It was getting to be a frequent chore of shoveling away the build up. Also odor was more than my wife and I wanted.

I visited a kennel where Beagles are kept off the ground in wire boxes above a concrete slab and the debris was washed into a septic tank. There were ten wired box cages with two dogs to a cage. This system seemed to work well but when finding out a good septic tank would cost around $1,000 I wondered if there were not a cheaper way to get the problem solved.

When reading my local paper one Sunday afternoon I read an article which told of earthworms being used in a landfill to break down organic matter. I reasoned that if they would be used on such a large scale then it just might be the answer that I had been looking for. I had learned from the time I was a small boy who really enjoyed fishing, that good fishing earthworms could be found along outdoor drainage lines from kitchen sinks. We did not have running water or indoor plumbing in those days, just sent unwanted waste down drainage ditches. A lot of people not living in those days have a hard time understanding how we managed. I admit one of the best things mankind has done is move the toilet indoors. It sure is nice to know that when there is something worth watching on TV that the toilet is just down the hall.

Since I still enjoy fishing I was purchasing some boxes of red wigglers and common local earthworms, also managing to find some night crawlers along a stream that runs through my farm. By adding earthworms to the back of my Rabbitmaster kennel, keeping the area moist from washing down the kennel there was been a build up of earthworms that has broken down the organic material behind the kennel to the point that I have not had to remove build up all during 2003. One thing that I find very interesting about the lowly earthworm is that each worm contains both sexes and when two worms mate, each fertilizes the other worm's eggs.

There may be a way to keep an earthworm population high enough to keep the build up down and sell off some fishing worms to the public. The area behind my kennel has been left undisturbed,d therefore I have no knowledge of how many earthworms are at work, only that I owe a lot to the lowly earthworm toward maintaining my Rabbitmaster hound kennel.

For those of you who did not read my article about my Rabbitmaster hounds in the February 2002 issue of The Rabbit Hunter magazine and you may be wondering what is a Rabbitmaster hound? This breed was developed by crossing the English Hunting Basset and the French Hunting Basset then breeding this cross to a full blooded high quality medium speed Beagle. The Beefmaster cattle breed is: ¼ Hereford, ¼ Shorthorn and ½ Brahman. The Rabbitmaster breed is ¼ English Basset, ¼ French (Petit Griffon Vendeen Basset) and ½ Beagle.

I enjoyed reading Mr. Stephen E. Tilmann's article in my Rabbit Hunter magazine about Edgar, a Basset in a Beagle's body. In the Rabbitmaster hound, the English Basset gives great voice, and a sense of smell. The French Basset (Fuzzie hair coat), has the amazing ability to find a rabbit and we all know how important that trail and the right type of Beagle cross really blends all the desirable good traits in making a top notch Rabbitmaster hound.

Ron Swanson, owner of a hunting Basset pack, brings his hound to my farm for training. They are well disciplined, hard hunters, and a great pleasure to listen to. Mr. Swanson showed me a French Basset he has received from a friend from Mississippi, who brought over some French Bassets from France. In France with the French Basset they run hare, stag and fox. The hunters decide what they want to hunt on a given day and that is what the dogs run. Mr. Swanson is finding out for me how they signal the hounds. My hunting buddy Walter Embrick tells me he had a bird dog that he trained to hunt quail and rabbits, and the dogs knew what he wanted to hunt for a given day.

With hunting season coming as it is now early in October, my Rabbitmaster hounds are ready to give me great hound music, and my started pups, Thunder and Lightning, are showing me they will do their part in some great rabbit races. The lowly earthworm has his eye focused on the thousands of oak leaves ready to fall and I feel strongly my pen's leaf accumulation will not become a problem.

No doubt, my Rabbitmaster hounds and the lowly earthworms work well together.

—published November 2003 in *The Rabbit Hunter*

Wiggles and the Rabbit Master Hounds
By Kenneth Bridges

No one knows where she came from. Wiggles appeared at our farm in October 2011, this little jet-black dog with a white chest and four white feet. She had a bob tail that she'd swing with a big wiggle. Our son David thus quickly named her "'Wiggles." She had no collar, but it was clear she was in top flesh condition with her beautiful shiny jet-black hair coat. Her friendliness was amazing and she quickly won our hearts. Subscribing to the *Full Cry* magazine, I noticed that Wiggles matched the characteristics of the Stephens breed. Wiggles also could be a Parnell Carolina Cur (Stephens/Feist Cross).

At the time of Wiggles' arrival, we had just lost our close house pet, an American Bulldog we had for twelve years. My granddaughter had recently lost her horse and it was very hard on her. My wife, Marilyn, and I gave her a card to let her know God always sends a replacement. What a wonderful replacement God sent with Wiggles.

I am a retired teacher of Agriculture now raising Polled Shorthorn cattle on my farm located in the rolling hills of Northeast Georgia. We live on a wooded lot with hardwoods that house lots of squirrels. Wiggles quickly took on the job of keeping the squirrels in their place, which she saw as the tops of the hardwoods. She accomplished this by chasing the foolish ones who ventured to the ground and then by standing on the tree trunk, barking to assure they reached their proper heights. In the 2013 *Full Cry,* Mr. Billy Price included a picture of Bruiser on a tree. That photo would pass for a photo of Wiggles doing her best.

Growing up in the 1940's, I started rabbit hunting around 6 years old with my dad, tracking rabbits in the snow. World War II was in progress and we were on food rations so wild game enabled my three brothers and I to make it to adulthood. Hunting dogs were a big part of my life on the farm as was plowing with mules, hoeing and picking cotton.

We took our mixed breed dogs to the fields with us in the mornings, and I got a lot of pleasure from listening to the rabbit and coon races while we did the hard physical work. I remember many cross-bred dogs that could really get the job done on a hunt.

In reading the history of the Stephens breed development, the breeding principles they used are the same as the ones I have used in the development of the Rabbitmaster breed. As a teacher of Agriculture teaching students livestock breeding principles, I saw that line breeding really works well with swine and beef cattle. Selecting for the traits you desire in an animal, be it cattle or dogs, is very important to achieve a desired product. The Beefmaster cattle breed was developed by using ¼ Hereford, ¼ Shorthorn and ½ Brahman. Each breed has things that you want in a good beef animal. This same breeding principle has been used to develop our modern-day breeds of swine.

The Rabbitmaster breed consists of ¼ Petit Basset Griffon Vendéen, ¼ Basset Bleu De Gascogne and ½ Beagle. The result is a hound with great voice, great sense of smell and the brains to run a rabbit hard. These two Basset breeds are two of the best hunting breeds developed in the country of France, and a lot of hunting breeds have been developed in that country. Two dog books that describe these two breeds are *Dogs* by Yann Arthus and *Schuster's Guide to Dogs* by Bertrand and Simon. Two Beagle lines I have been using are Weir Creek and Warfield Red. Currently, I am using Outcross strain, Phillip Greenbrier BL Jack, Colar Bluetick and Black & Tan. I feel sure the French hunting Bassets would also cross well with other good breeding stock.

Wildlife experts tell us there are eight species of cottontail rabbits that blanket the United States, Canada and Mexico. On my farm in Northeast Georgia, we have the good fortune of having the big swamp rabbit we call "Cane Cutters." To me, after 75 years of rabbit hunting, the Cane Cutter is the one species that can put a pack of rabbit hounds to a real test. The Cane Cutter lives in the swamp and runs dogs through all the water and mud available in his immediate environment.

Wiggles is an enthusiastic hunting machine who has shown great aptitude at jumping rabbits for my pack. When I start putting on my hunting clothes, she gets excited, jumping up and down and spinning in circles. While hunting with the Rabbitmasters, she is everywhere at once, looking for rabbits no matter what the terrain conditions might be.

Often I stop to check the squirrel she has treed as a side project of the hunt. When we return home from the rabbit hunt, she starts stalking out the yards, making sure we know that she is still in the squirrel hunting business.

In my 75 years having owned many smart, intelligent dogs I don't believe I have had a smarter, more versatile one than Wiggles. She is an excellent housedog and loyal pet. Wiggles treats all of our farm visitors with high respect. Above all, Wiggles is a hard-hitting hunting dog that loves a good outing with the Rabbitmaster hounds. The Lord blessed my family well when he provided us with a dog named "Wiggles."

—published 2004 in *The Rabbit Hunter*

The Ghost and the Rabbitmaster Hounds
By Kenneth R. Bridges

Ghost—As a very young boy, I was introduced to what people called a "ghost" in several different ways.

I remember a very frightening night when I was eight years old. Being in bed alone as my little brother, Ben, was away visiting. The month was late August and all the windows were open. The hot Georgia nights were beginning to get a chill, late in the evening. My mother had placed a light blanket across the foot of our bed in case we felt the chill. It was about 2-3 o'clock in the morning, and I reached for my blanket. Sitting up in bed, I felt what I thought was a human arm. Thinking to myself, "If this is a human arm, then there must be a hand.' I moved my hand down the arm, sure enough, there was a hand with fingers as still as the arm. A deep horror gripped me in my stomach that I will never forget. Trying hard to call my parents, no sound would come. My voice was dead with fear. A cold feeling came over me like I have never known. I must have blacked out only to awake at daylight to find the window still open, but the screen wire that covered the window gone. My Mother and Dad assured me that I was in no danger. They told me it was just the ghost of old Ben Allan known for years to walk the road by our house, and on occasion would stop in to pay a visit to people he liked. Since that time, I have seen and heard lots of ghosts. I always think of the hand I felt in bed that night when someone says, "Are you in good hands?"

There was another time when I was fourteen years old with three young brothers, Ben 12, Thomas 10, and Robert 8. The Georgia Power Company decided to construct a big line across our land. They built a dam across the creek over which they drove their equipment. All of us boys really enjoyed fishing, and with the water backed up, nightfall would find us fishing late into the night much to our parents' dismay. Late one night when at our age we should have been in bed, we heard what we all perceived to be a ghost. About 200 yards away a blood curdling scream pierced the night. "Kenneth, let's go home," all three brothers pleaded. I had just landed a nice mud catfish, so though blood was running cold in my veins, "Keep fishing," I replied, "whatever it is will go away." As you might know, I was not to have that kind of luck on that fishing trip. No sooner had I made my brave statement then the same blood curdling scream came again only about 100 yards closer. I have been watching the Olympics and we could have finished 1st, 2nd , 3rd and 4th in some of those races if they had been held at our farm that night. It was about one mile to our house and we arrived in about four minutes, with fear all over our faces. We told our parents we had heard the scream of a "woman ghost." They assured us we had heard the scream of Ghost Ann Minish, who was murdered twenty years ago in the oak woods just above where we were fishing. Ghost Ann ended our night fishing on Hardman Creek.

Now to prepare you for some of a most daring "ghost happening" a little Rabbitmaster hound information is recorded.

With only three inches total rain for March through May, the first two weeks of June brought nine inches. The briars and undergrowth really got thick and when I took the Rabbitmasters out to chase Br. Rabbit the going was tough. Multiflower Rose, thistle, bramble briars, kudzu, you name int and I can just assure you it can be found in Northeast Georgia.

In late Spring and Summer some of my hunting buddies brought their rabbit hunting dog packs to hunt on my farm. Here on the farm we have two types of wild rabbits, cottontails, Swamper and cane cutter, also know as Buck Rabbit. South Georgia has the Marsh Rabbit, also known as the blue belly rabbit. I have always wondered could my Rabbitmaster Hounds run the Northern Hare? And how does our Swamper compare to the Northern Hare? My good friend, Mr. Ted Martin, up in Uniontown, PA, will answer my first question. Mr. Martin has bought a mature trained Rabbitmaster hound from me. This dog, Walt, nicknamed Chubby, and I made him live up to his name by keeping him fifteen pounds overweight. In checking with Ted he tells me he has removed those fifteen pounds and that Chubby is really driving cottontails like a good hound should. Ted will let me know if he can run on snow and drive the Northern Hare. To answer my second question, I contacted Dr. Larry Marchinton, Wildlife Specialist at the University of Georgia, Athens. Dr. Marchinton now retired, did deer and rabbit research for years. It was always a thrill for my Vo. Ag. Students to visit the deer research projects being conducted by Dr. Marchinton. Larry showed me examples of different stuffed rabbit species hanging in a row on the wall of his wildlife room in his home. A Hare he killed in Wisconsin, Swamper he killed locally, cottontail and Marsh Rabbit. The Swamper was slightly larger than the Hare and cottontail. Marsh about the same size. Dr. Marchinton sure knows his deer and rabbits. He is also known far and wide for his outstanding rabbit running Beagle Packs. Dr. Marchinton is the type of man someone like myself could spend hours talking to about rabbit hunting.

There were several great races given by several rabbit running packs this year on my farm. However, there seems to be a strange ghostly happening near the creek that runs through a swamp in the middle of my farm. It seemed at the same location in the thick brush on a hill above the creek, different rabbit running packs would jump something and take it full cry, down across the creek. There would be a short run in the swamp, then silence. The race was over. This happened to my friend's packs quite a few times. They were very puzzled. I remembered Ghost Ann, "Could she be involved in some way?" No one could find a hole and rabbits don't actually go to ground that quick especially in that type of cover. I am sure some of you are thinking that Ghost Ann's scream was the mating call of a Bobcat and our Ghost was a Bobcat going up a tree.

Hunting near the ghostly happening that was taking place on two occasions, my Rabbitmasters gave me that same short full cry race then silence. When I say full cry of Rabbitmaster hounds, that means the hounds are running with great volume, a blend of beautiful voices like that of some gospel quartets. In the Rabbitmaster pack of seven, there is Hostess, a Foundation brood bitch for the Rabbitmaster breed. She is ½ English hunting Basset and ½ French Basset (Petit Griffon Vendeen). Hostess has a nice chop soprano. There is Velvet, Full Rabbitmaster, who is ¼ French, ¼ English Basset and ½ Beagle. She helps Hostess with the soprano. Full Rabbitmaster female, Lightning, cries with a deep great alto. However, things are not complete without the male parts. Thunder, a 2½ year old Full Rabbitmaster cry, is bass. A deeper, higher volume cry on a dog I have never heard. Thunder makes the ground vibrate. Buckeye, Full Bluetick Beagle that I am using for my Foundation male for the Rabbitmaster breed, cries baritone. He has a deep pleasing voice. Also there is my Full Red colored Beagle named Red, of course. Red supplies a beautiful tenor. I have just added a Full Warfield Red Beagle named Old Yellow. You see, a great rabbit hunting buddy of mine whose health has failed him, so Mr. Edward Glenn's doctor has advised him to let his dogs go. Mr. Glenn made 9 year old Yellow available to me. He has a very high pitch bell sounding voice, so I have assigned him to cry high tenor.

Two weeks ago, I took the Rabbitmaster hounds to the swamp in search of the Ghost. After releasing the hounds on the hill above the swamp, I hurried to a knoll on the creek bank that would allow me to watch the creek for a long stretch up stream. It took about ten minutes for the Rabbitmasters to strike and to really make some sweet hound music, driving hard toward the creek. As I watched closely, hoping to get a glimpse of this Ghost thing, one of the biggest Swamp Rabbits that I have ever seen crossed the creek in overdrive. The big "Swamper" took the hounds through some shallow ponds, then doubled back to the creek. I watched as the "swamper" leaped off the creek bank into the middle of the creek, and with only its nose above the water, he came swimming with the current down the middle of the creek. The "swamper" stayed in the middle of the creek swimming on past me and vanished like a Ghost that will appear to run another day. The Rabbitmaster hounds came full cry to the creek bank, then silence. They searched up and down both sides of the creek bank without luck for the scents. The Swamp Rabbit had tricked the hounds. Their beautiful chorus had ended.

Rabbit hunting season is coming to Georgia, and I have retired from teaching Agriculture in high school. For those who read my article in the Rabbit Hunter Magazine November 2003, "Rabbitmaster Hounds and the lowly Earthworms," I can inform you that the Earthworms have taken care of eliminating the waste accumulation at the back of my kennel. They have their eyes focused on the leaves above, soon to fall. As for me, I look forward to a lot of great Rabbitmaster hound music and you can bet we plan to run the Ghost.

—published January 2005 in *The Rabbit Hunter*

Basset Bleu Gascogne Rabbitmaster Hounds
By Kenneth R. Bridges

I received a call from my friend, Mr. Rod Swanson, one
Saturday wanting to know if I wanted to go with him to run
his rabbit hounds? I answered with a big "yes!" He is the
keeper and trainer of foxhounds for a large group of Atlanta
fox hunters. Raising and training hunting dogs has been his
life's occupation. Any hunter who knows Rod, be he a
feather or fur hunter, will tell you he is an excellent judge of
fox, rabbit and quail hunting dogs. The big thing to me is the
vast number of different hunting breeds he has worked with
over time. If the dog is good, no matter what hunting breed,
Rod will use him in the breeding program.

As we were loading the hounds, Rod introduced me
to a French Hunting Basset Bleu De Gascogne male. This
hound was about 13" tall, coat blue speckled with white with
extreme black markings and a trace of shading on the eyes
and cheeks. He stood on a great set of legs that looked to be
made for hours of hard running. He briefly mentioned that I
might want to use him in my Rabbitmaster breeding program.
The Rabbitmaster breed is ¼ French Hunting Basset, ¼
English Hunting Basset and ½ Beagle. For the French part, I
have been using the Petit Griffon Fendeen (Fuzzie Basset),
and have been very pleased with results.

Our hunt was to take place in a 200-acre high fenced
enclosure near Dawsonville, GA. The pack was pushing Mr.
Cottontail hard when from the thick brush I heard a hound
with a beautiful thundering voice. When I asked Mr.
Swanson, "What dog is that?" he replied, "This is the Basset
Bleu De Cascogne." I don't shoot many rabbits, as I hunt for
the beautiful hound music. When I heard the voice the dog
possessed, I knew he would fit my Rabbitmaster Hound

program. When I asked Rod how he came by that dog, he told me his sire was brought into Canada to run hare and he was to get a Bleu De Gascogne pup. Rod had promised to let Mr. Earnest Carlisle in South Carolina, who was familiar with the Bleu De Gascogne breed, use him on an outstanding Bluetick Beagle female. This meant that I must wait in line to use this great hunting dog in my program. As fate would have it, the Bleu De Gascogne male was killed by a car while being hunted, and Mr. Carlisle became ill and passed away. Rod did manage to obtain for me two Bleu De Gascogne Blue Tick Beagle crossed females from Mr. Carlisle's breeding program.

Beginning in March 2005, the Bleu De Gascogne breed was introduced into my Rabbitmaster hound pack. It wasn't long before the two were contributing greatly to the pack, pushing big Swamp Buck rabbits hard through swamp water, mud and multi-flower rosebushes. My hunting pal of many years, Mr. Walter Embrick, whose picture appeared on page 33, February 2002 issue of *The Rabbit Hunter* had great pleasure listening to the races. In late April, he became seriously ill and was confined to a hospital bed. Using an Olympus Pearl Condor 8702 (min-tape recorder), I recorded several Buck Rabbit races that I played for him at the hospital. Mr. Embrick passed away in June 2005 and was followed in death by his wife, Mary exactly to the day one month later. Another friend of mine, Mr. Edward Glyn told me he could play a tape of a rabbit race and his dogs would show up for loading when it came time to go home. My old dog, Buckeye's health was failing at the age of 12 years. It was Buckeye, whom I used for my foundation of the Rabbitmaster program. Buckeye had a voice any dog hunter would enjoy listening to on a rabbit run. I recorded Buckeye several times before he died.

October 2005 came with my looking forward to a great hunting season with the Rabbitmaster hounds, but the unexpected happened. Starting with what was thought to be kidney stone attacks was found to be cancer in my right kidney. My bad kidney was removed in December 2005 and while in recovery for 6 weeks I did not see the Rabbitmaster, but I really enjoyed the recorded rabbit races.

Did you ever see someone rabbit hunt from a golf cart? I never thought of giving up rabbit hunting for golf, but during my recovery, I got to hear hounds from a golf cart. Mr. Maxie Skinner of Demorest, GA has a large group of good gun dog hunting Beagles. Mr. Skinner a retired coach, has trouble with his legs and has recruited two of his former basketball players to handle his hounds. Maxie invited me on a cold day in February 2006 to ride in the cart with him. I was really amazed how well we followed the hounds with the golf cart and the number of rabbits we bagged from the cart with his 410 gauge shotgun.

Something new that really works, common sense says it should be tried, like using the golf cart, the min-recorder and introducing the French Basset Bleu De Gascogne into the Rabbitmaster breed. These are three things I am pleased to have tried.

Back in 1930, Tom Lasater of Falfurrias, TX developed the Beefmaster breed of cattle by crossing the Braham, Shorthorn and Hereford breeds. His goal was to blend the desired best qualities of each breed into a breed of superior cattle. This breed is very popular in the South today. My goals with the Rabbitmaster breed is the same as Tom Lasater's goal. With the French Bassets, I have found the answer to finding the rabbit and to finding the ability to push the rabbit hard using a great sense of smell. They say the sense of smell ability of a Basset is second only to a Bloodhound and a high volume voice that gives great pleasure to listen to on the trail. This is a rabbit dog that can run under tough conditions with a strong desire to catch the rabbit. Hybrid vigor has been found to be very desirable characteristic in animal breeding. An example is, after breeding six litters of Rabbitmasters in cold winter conditions, not a pup was lost! When breeding pure bred Beagles, losing pups is common. Please feel free to call me at [706-768-3480] if you would like to know more about the Rabbitmaster breed.

—published July 2006 in *The Rabbit Hunter*

Canecutters and Rabbitmaster Hounds in Hi-Definition
By Kenneth R. Bridges

Rabbit hunting fever was instilled in me by my dad at a very young age. Ralph Bridges taught me to track rabbits in the snow, and how to hunt Cottontails and Canecutters with mixed breeds of dogs. After school when farm work was done, I would grab my single barrel shotgun (during hunting season) for a quick hunt before dark.

Hunting season in Georgia for rabbit is from November 12-February 28 with a limit of 12 rabbits daily. However, if you shoot many daily limits, having all the many rabbit predators, you would soon be out of rabbits to hunt. My passion for rabbit hunting comes in listening and watching a good pack of hounds work. I have not shot a rabbit in years as dead rabbits do not provide beautiful music. I spent a career of 43 years teaching Agriculture in high school. I started a herd of registered Polled Shorthorns in 1966 and still work with my cattle herd in 2007. However, for the past 10 years I have been working on developing a superior breed of rabbit hounds that I call my Rabbitmasters. This breed is a cross using two French hunting Bassets crossed with one-half Beagle. The French breeds are: Petite Basset Griffon Vendeen and Basset Bleu De Gascogne. These two breeds are two of the best rabbit hunting hounds developed in the country of France, and a lot of hunting breeds have been developed in that country. Two dog books that describe these two breed are Dogs by Yann, Arthus and Bertrand and Simon and Schuscter's Guide to Dogs. I really got interested in hunting dogs when studying those dog books. The Rabbitmaster is ¼ Petite Basset Griffon Vendeen, ¼ Basset Blue De Gascogne, and ½ Beagle. The result is a hound with great voice, sense of smell, brains, and stamina to run hard – a big Canecutter Rabbit. Two strains of

Beagle lines I have been using in this cross are Weir Creek and Warfield Red. I am sure the French Hunting Bassets would cross well with other good breeding hunting stock.

In February, William and Mandy Bobbitt, owners of the Bedlam Beagles from Rockbridge, VA, came to Georgie to visit the Rodney Swansons of Nowhere Farm Foot Hound. So, they also brought their private pack of Beagles to my farm. A dozen local rabbit hunters showed up to watch their private packs in action. Mr. Terry Smith, my Baptist Pastor who is an avid rabbit hunter, was among the group. After some great Cottontail races, we moved to the big swamp and a big Canecutter was jumped. There are no Canebutters where the Bobbits live in Virginia and even though they had no experience dealing with the mud and water, the Canecutter baptized them in – they did quite well! The problem came when it was time to load their Beagles for home, they were so covered with mud it was hard to tell the Bobbit's and Swanson's dogs apart.

Wildlife experts tell us there are eight species of Cottontails that blanket the United States, Canada, and Mexico. They thrive in a variety of habitat types from coastal marsh to desert. On my farm located in the northeast corner of Georgia, we have the good fortune to have the big swamp rabbits we call a Canebutter. This species of wild rabbit has a big bag of tricks he can use to elude predators. To me, after sixty years of rabbit hunting, the Canecutter is the one rabbit that can really put a pack of rabbit hounds to the real test.

In the 1960s, the U.S. Government started building water shed lakes on small streams for flood control. As part of this building project, small streams were dredged eliminating natural ponds in swamps where the Canecutter lived. Back then I only found this Canecutter in very poorly drained swamps along the larger streams. However, he has adapted to change in a remarkable way. Today I find the

Canecutter on small streams, around small ponds, and evidence he now ranges on hillsides. The evidence I speak of is the way you can tell if there are Canecutters at a location. Unlike the cottontail, who puts his waste droppings on the ground, the Canecutter will deposit his waste droppings on top of stumps, logs, and even on top of Fire Ant hills. He goes in this location more than once. The Canecutter runs the hounds through all the deep mud and water available. His best trick is to get in a stream with his nose above water and float a long way down before exiting the stream. If all else fails, he will take to a stump, hollow tree, or log piles, but this won't be necessary often, as he is one intelligent critter that believes he can out think and outlast any good pack of Rabbit Hounds. One thing that I really like about the Canecutter is that he can take the Rabbitmasters out of hearing and back, if the dogs really stay close.

Sitting at my television watching the local news cast one day (after some great Canecutter races) the news anchor informed me that he was bringing me the news in "Hi-Definition." I did not really understand what he was eluding to, but decided whatever he meant, it must be very good. A friend of mine explained to me that I would have to purchase a special type T.V. to get strong up close results that "Hi-Definition" gives. It occurred to me that was what I was getting when watching and listening to my Rabbitmaster Hounds driving hard a big Canecutter rabbit!

A good friend of mine, Mr. Dillard Owenby, has a 20 acre starting pen. A lot of hunters bring their field trial dogs and pups for him to train. Dillard also has some top-notch AKC registered Beagles trained to really drive a rabbit. I really enjoy listening to his hounds and greatly appreciate his help with my Rabbitmasters. One day Dillard asked me if he could come listen to my Rabbitmasters run a Canecutter. Telling him I would really enjoy his company, I forgot to tell him to be sure to wear his rubber boots because a lot of water would be involved. Dillard was standing on the dry side of the creek and the Rabbitmasters were really pouring it on Mr. Canecutter in the bottom on the oppose side of the creek. They were what we country boys call letting the "hammer down." Without worrying about wet feet, he crossed the creek wearing his leather shoes as he wanted to see and hear this rabbit race in "Hi-Definition."

One morning in late January 2007, I took my Vendeen Rabbitmasters: Thunder, Lightning, and Velvet, my great jump Rabbitmaster, plus my three Blue De Gascogne Rabbtmasters: Peaches, Cream, and Midnight to the Canecutter swamp. Velvet quickly started a big Canecutter and the hounds music was really in Hi-Definition, as I stood in the middle of the big swamp listening to and watching the big rabbit go effortlessly through the mud and water passing by me three times. The race ended finely about 50 yards away. A small sub-stream flows through the swamp flowing back to the main creek bed. In a very short time Peaches found Mr. Canecutter resting in the sub-stream and the race was on again. Peaches has a beautiful fast chop mouth and I've read stories about hunting dogs with the chop mouths who could really smell a rabbit. My question is, "Do dogs with the chop mouths really have the best noses?" I have only had three chop mouth hounds and they all could really find the rabbit. One of my chop mouth dogs, Hostess, caught too many rabbits in the bed, thus no good rabbit races. Anyway, after Peaches found Mr. Canecutter in the sub-stream, he had had enough, so he headed for a big pile of logs and burying deep under them. Peaches, Cream, Lightning and Old Yellow, my twelve year old Warfield Red Beagle that still has what it takes to drive a rabbit hard, were determined to dig him out. This Canecutter I wanted to live another day, so with my leads and much effort, I managed to get them from the log pile. One Canecutter tried to outrun the Rabbitmasters, his luck ran out, he was caught. I took a picture of this rabbit with Peaches and Cream checking him out as I held the rabbit. This picture I am sending to The Rabbit Hunter magazine.

You could say my second career is working with my rabbit dogs. Nothing I enjoy more than training the Rabbitmasters. At present, I am expecting a litter of pups, a cross between Cream and Old Yellow were due April 12, 2007. Next on my training list are six months old yellow and white male pups, named Mello Yellow and Little Red. I am counting on them to carry on Old Yellow's blood in my breeding program.

If you want to try your dogs on Canecutters, feel free to give me a call at 706-757-3908. Bring rubber boots.

—published June 2007 in *The Rabbit Hunter*

My Experience Breeding Shorthorn in Georgia

(50 Years)

Kenneth Bridges

Growing up as a boy in the later 1940s, my three brothers and I plowed mules, picked cotton and cared for livestock on the family farm while my parents worked in a textile mill.

My first experience with a Shorthorn was as a student enrolled in Vocational Agriculture and participating as an FFA member at Commerce High School in Commerce, Georgia. My Vo-Ag. Teacher, Mr. Roy Powell wanted me to buy and grow out a Shorthorn steer. The price of the animal was $300.00, which was much more than my parents could afford. They were able to purchase me an Angus steer for $100.00. I don't believe that calf had seen too many humans. Mr. Powell was a large, strong man, with three other men to help but the steer nearly flipped the FFA Chapter truck when they loaded the animal to take to our farm. I fed the steer through the cracks in our log barn, until I was able to go inside his stall to feed and eventually break him to a halter. The steer trusted me but would object to anyone else holding his halter. I told the Judge at the FFA Chapter Show the steer would kick him if he came too close, but he learned this himself upon approaching the animal. A member of our chapter brought the Shorthorn steer; a calm, great calf that won the show.

Commerce, Georgia in the early 1950s was a small town. They had just built the Andrew Jackson Hotel, which was two stories, but I had not been inside it. This is the hotel where Bill Anderson wrote the country music hit, "City Lights." In my 10th grade year, my Vo-Ag teacher told us that we were going to Atlanta. This is when I first had a chance to go inside a hotel. The walls in the Biltmore Hotel on Ponce de Leon Avenue were trimmed in velvet, like my Grandma's

Sunday Hat. In the corner of what they called the 'Lobby' was a box-shaped small room, with a door that opened smoothly. A man with a fancy suit stood inside at a control module. As we watched an old woman strolled across the Lobby, entered into the box, the door closed and the box rose up through the ceiling. My Ag Teacher with the rest of us teenagers watched at presently the box lowered back down through the ceiling and a beautiful, young, red-haired lady emerged and strolled through the Lobby and out the front doors. I asked Mr. Powell what was this contraption, and he replied, "I don't know, but I'm going home to get my wife and let her go up and down a few times." I decided strongly in the 10th grade I was going to become a Vo-Ag. Teacher.

My high school graduation year was 1955. By this time, I had a subscription to the 'Shorthorn World' magazine. I have maintained my subscription to that magazine continuously. In my high school years in Georgia, there were Angus, Hereford and Shorthorn breeds available. I still have in my possession the October 15, 1955 edition of 'Shorthorn World,' which shows cattle pictured with very deep bodies, short legs and short, well-shaped horns. They were typically heavy fat carriers. A one-year subscription to the magazine in 1955 was $2.00 U.S and $2.50 Canadian. The Shorthorn World Publishing Company, 16 South Locust Street, Aurora, Illinois published the magazine twice a month. Many of the Shorthorn farms listed back then are no longer around today. However, I did find some recognizable names like 'Sutherland, Leveldale, Ashbourne' and the Leemon Stock Farm. The Leveldale Investment Sale Catalog was included in the October 15,

1955 issue. The sale was held on November 5, 1955 in Aurora, Illinois. Mr. Hal Longley was the Sale Manager for this sale, as he was for many other sales listed in that issue of Shorthorn World.

After obtaining a bachelor's degree in Agricultural Education from the University of Georgia, I started my career at Union County High School in Blairsville, Georgia as a Vo-Ag teacher. This beautiful area was located on the Tennessee and North Carolina borders, with new crops and livestock I was unaccustomed to. This is where I had my first experience with sheep at the University of Georgia Mountain Agricultural Experiment Station.

The Union County FFA Chapter had never shown cattle before my arrival but I found several members interested in the prospect of showing steers. No heifers were shown during this era. After a very successful 5 years teaching in Union County, Mr. Walter Nix, the Vo-Ag. teacher of neighboring Towns County took the Principal's position and made it worth my while to come teach Agriculture in his high school. We had a very strong FFA Show String of steers in Union County. Most of the steers were Shorthorn. In the North Georgia Mountains there were some very good Shorthorn breeders. Knowing how much the opportunity to take a calf to show had influenced my decision to become a Vo-Ag. teacher, I continued to build on the Town County Show Team. This chapter had shown cattle at the Georgia Mountain Fair in Hiawassee, Georgia but never at the State Cattle Show. With the help of local Shorthorn breeders, Mr. E. J. Whitmire of Franklin, North Carolina and Mr. Rueben Walls of Hiawassee, Georgia, the Towns County FFA Chapter was able to submit a Shorthorn Exhibit to the State Cattle Show held in Macon, Georgia.

There was no ready mixed steer feed available in our area, so we made trips to where I grew up in Commerce, Georgia to obtain oats to mix with the corn that was readily available in the North Georgia Mountains. I remember holding an adult class on feeding swine. The feed salesman I had invited to help with the class asked if I had anyone who only fed their hogs table scraps. I took him to meet a boy's dad that only would allow the boy to feed his show pig slop. The feed salesman asked the dad how long it took to get the pig to 200 pounds. He replied that if he started feeding in March he could have him to that weight by killing time in November. The salesman told the boy's dad, "what would you say if I told you I could sell you a feed that could get your hog to 200 pounds in half that time?" The man thought for a moment and said, "What's time to a hog?"

While still teaching in Towns County I had the chance to buy the 150-acre cotton farm I grew up on in 1962. It took me four years to build fences and change the cotton fields to grass. I knew what grew best on those fields was grass. As a boy, we had to plow the mules hard and keep the hoes moving to keep the grass out of our cotton.

Being sold on Shorthorns and now with fences and grass, I purchased my first cattle. The purchase consisted of 6 cows and one polled bull on July 4, 1966. Starting with 3 cows, 3 heifers and a bull my first 12 calves born were heifers. I know God was helping me get a Shorthorn herd started. In 1967 while still teaching in Hiawassee, Georgia, I took 6 Shorthorn steers to Albany, Georgia. This was a 300-mile, one-way trip with the cattle on the back of a 2-ton truck. This was all 2 lane, rural roads and no Interstate. We then took the 6 steers two weeks later to the Georgia State Show in Macon, Georgia. One of our animals was picked as the Shorthorn State Champion Steer.

In 1968, I had an opportunity to take a job as the Vo-Ag. teacher in Oconee County High School located in Watkinsville, Georgia. This was 4 miles South of the University of Georgia located in Athens, Georgia, where I had earned my Bachelor's Degree. As in the Union County FFA Chapter, no one was showing beef cattle when I became the Vo-Ag. teacher in Oconee County. In my first year of teaching, we began showing beef cattle. Shorthorns were a big part of our Show String, but we did include other breeds. Being located close to UGA, I started working on my Graduate Degree in Agricultural Education, which I completed in 1972.

To get up enough Shorthorn show cattle and to develop my Shorthorn breeding herd, I had to travel to farms in Tennessee, South Carolina and other States. Herds that I and my FFA members visited in the late 1960's were: Waukaru in Indiana, L.E. Eichenberger in Tennessee, Randy Griffis in Pendleton, South Carolina, Sutherland Farms in Prospect, Kentucky, Gay & Emory Shurley in Warrington, Georgia, Charles Curtis in Cookeville, Tennessee, Charles Hix in Cowan, Tennessee, Dedom Farms in North Carolina, T. Elias McGee in South Carolina, R. Lee Johnson in Ohio and Jack Dobbins in South Carolina.

By the year 1973, my Shorthorn herd had grown to 43 brood cows. The American Shorthorn Association sent me a plaque stating I was the top Georgia Shorthorn recorded for that year. In the same year, I was asked to judge the Tennessee National Sale held in Nashville, Tennessee. During this time, I was teaching vocational agriculture to adult students at night. Some of my students had begun to take notice of my Shorthorn cattle and asked for my help to start their own herds. One of the farmers wanted to know where we could find some 'sho-nuff' good bulls. I thought the 1971 National Polled Congress would be the right place. We hitched a 16' cattle trailer to a 1970 Buick, and with Mr. Rueben Walls from Hiawassee, Georgia, we went to the National Polled Congress held in Louisville, Kentucky. At this sale, we purchased the Polled Congress Champion, *Scarcliffe Royal Cloud* from Questing Hills Farm out of Chandlerville, Illinois for Mr. Alan Hudson from Athens, Georgia for $3150.00. Alan Hudson also bought *Nector of Ashborne*, from Ashbourne Farms located in LeGrange, Kentucky along with *J. F. Camon Dandy* from Fieser, Kansas. Rueben Walls purchased *Bonnivue Max Leader 13+* from 5M Farms out of Fairfield, Texas. *Nector of Ashbourne* sired the 1979 Georgia State Champion Steer.

It is a fact that we bought more bulls at the National Polled Congress than our 16' trailer could hold. We sent the Fiser bull home with a breeder from Franklin, North Carolina and took the other 3 bulls over the mountains between Franklin and Hiawassee in the middle of the night. Rueben Walls lived 1/2 mile off the main road and the Buick was challenged to pull such a load up a steep dirt road. He was not deterred, and happily led his new Texas bull home in the dark, by halter. Our Congress Bull buying trip was a great success except the Buick needed a new set of brakes once we got home.

One of my fellow Georgia Vo-Ag. teachers, who liked another breed of beef cattle, started kidding me about having Shorthorns. I told him that over 30 breeds of cattle had Shorthorn blood, only his breed could not claim kinship to Shorthorn because they did not produce enough milk. At an Ag. Teachers conference he got me up in front of fellow teachers and told them what I had said, and that I was teaching wrong. The very next month, the Southern Beef Producers Magazine published an article on breeds of beef cattle. The magazine said in their article that over 30 breeds of beef cattle held Shorthorn lineage. We had an update at our next Ag. Teacher's conference on the value of

Shorthorns. I have a copy of this article and it referenced the Food and Agriculture Organization of the United Nations.

It was an honor for me to be asked to judge the Pre-Sale Show for the 1974 Tennessee Show Sale. According to the Show Sale write up, this proved to be one of the better consignment sales in North America, with a very large crowd attending. I was pleased that the Champion Bull, *Elma Villa Munster II,* consigned by Carl Jordan was the high seller - sold to Clifton, Kentucky for $1500.00. Also, the Champion Female, *Nelco Wily Lilly II* was the high selling female for $1000.00.

All throughout the 1960s and 1970s cattle breeders wanted larger frame, faster growing cattle and the duel-purpose Shorthorns were just the answer. Popular bulls at that time were *Kenmar Ramson* and *Ball Dee Perfect Count.*

As a Vo-Ag. teacher with FFA students showing lots of Shorthorn heifers, we needed to breed them to top AI bulls. I learned how to AI breed so I could breed my student's heifers at no cost. I kept an AI tank and ordered semen from top bulls. This kept down shipping costs for students.

I took many of my students to the National FFA Convention in Kansas City, Missouri. While on one of these trips to Kansas City, I got to see the American Royal Cattle Show and see the iconic bulls, *Deerpark Improver* and *Deerpark Dividend.* Dividend was born March 9, 1973 and had a 205-day weight of 810 pounds (no creep). Mr. Bob Houser, my District FFA Livestock Teacher viewed these animals with me and stated, "Well, they are just big bulls." (He was an Angus breeder). Now, in the year 2016, we know the great effect these two bulls had on the Shorthorn breed.

Starting in the early 1960s, the exotic breeds of cattle from Europe starting to arrive in the U.S. My first experience with them was when I was the Livestock Supervisor at the Georgia Mountain Fair Livestock Show held in Hiawassee, Georgia every year. A man from Blue Ridge, Georgia had purchased some Charolais, which he had brought for display at the fair. The Charolais had more size for age and more muscle than our Angus, Herefords and Shorthorns. I have in my library a book on breeds of cattle, written by Herman R. Purdy. If you need to know cattle breeds, this book is hard to beat. If you need to know Shorthorns, the two books by Otis Fisher, *Shorthorns Around the World* and *The Story of Milking Shorthorns in the U.S.* are excellent resources to own.

At the International Livestock Exposition honoring 75 years of shows in Chicago with 128 head in the ring, the Shorthorn exhibit was the largest of all breeds. The Champion Bull was 'Millbrook Ransom G-9, shown by Bob-Lee and R. E. Johnson. Judge for the show was Roger Hunley. He demanded size in his champions with as much length and muscling as he could find, being critical of over finish and structural unsoundness, particularly of feet and legs.

Due to the concerns about fat causing heart health problems, the 1960s and 1970s moved toward bigger, taller and leaner framed cattle. I know the big dual-purpose Shorthorns could help, and we could add muscle with the Irish and Maine-Anjou bloodlines. When we could use Shorthorn Appendix Registration, I took advantage of it. However, when we switched to calling them Shorthorn Plus, it took three years to get our State Show FFA/4-H show officials to understand that a change had been made.

In order to cross my Irish Shorthorns and the dual-purpose Milking Shorthorns, I also subscribe to the Milking Shorthorn magazine. The Paul Ragan Herd located in Monticello, Florida was my first herd to visit. I was deeply impressed with this herd. They had been brought from Nebraska, when Mr. Ragan started his herd. There was one cow in this herd that was the most impressive cow I had ever seen of any breed. Paul called her 'High Pockets', officially named, 'Ridgecrest Maria IV.' Some time later I visited Carl and Barry Jordan of Warukara Farms and told them about Ridgecrest Maria IV. Mr. Ragan was killed in a tragic train accident and the Jordans purchased 'High Pockets' at auction to use in their embryo transplant program. Even though she was 12 years old, she produced many champions for them. Barry Jordan told me after their success with Ridgecrest Maria that, "cream always rises to the top." I have to agree with that.

In the middle 1970s and early 1980s, several of my Oconee County cattlemen wanted me to help them get what they called 'Milking Shorthorns.' I made trips to Elmer Von Tunglin's 'Clayside Farm' in Verdan, Oklahoma. I also made trips to the Sandy River-York Farm in Farmington, Maine. Altogether, we purchased around 25 head form these farms. Sires represented were 'Defender Promise' and 'New Park Gay King.'

In 1967, my wife Mary Ellen and I were blessed with a son we named Starling Kenneth Bridges. In 1969, we were again blessed with a daughter, whom we named Shannon Marella. This meant we would hope to have our children to be part of our Shorthorn program and have the opportunity to show our cattle in 4-H and FFA shows in the local area. When Starling and Shannon were small; 3 and 6 years old, we had a very gentle roan Shorthorn cow that produced excess milk for her calf. She would let them milk her with only a feed bucket to keep her occupied. She never kicked or even moved while they were milking. 'Strawberry' was a great cow that exhibited the gentleness of the Shorthorn breed.

Starling and Shannon both started showing Shorthorns when they were old enough to be in 4-H. Being two years older than

Shannon, Starling got a head start on learning how to show a calf. I remember at one show they were both entering into the Showmanship competition with their Shorthorn heifers. Before going into the show ring, Shannon said, "Daddy, I don't know what to do and won't do well." I told her to just watch her brother and do what he does. The judge placed Shannon ahead of Starling that day in Showmanship.

Both Starling and Shannon did well showing Shorthorn heifers and steers. At the Georgia Junior State Heifer Show in 1982, Starling showed the State Champion Shorthorn Heifer and Shannon showed the State Reserve Champion Shorthorn Heifer. K&M's 'Show Starr' appeared in the December 1982 Shorthorn Country magazine. It stated, "Show Starr, exhibited by her owner, Starling Bridges from Athens, Georgia has been a consistent winner and was recently named Supreme Champion over 120 head from eight different breeds and has been chosen Champion Female twice in inter-breed competition. She was by 'McKee's PA Beau' and was bred by Harold Martin of Carnesville, Georgia.

Georgia Junior
STATE HEIFER SHOW

As the number of Shorthorn heifers and steers greatly increased at the regional livestock shows, a number of Shorthorn breeders wanted to form the State's first Georgia Shorthorn Association. This was done in 1984. The Association started offering the incentive award of $500.00 for the Georgia Champion Shorthorn Heifer and $250.00 for the Reserve Champion Shorthorn Heifer at the State Show held in Perry, Georgia every year. We as Shorthorn breeders felt a need to increase the number of shows in Georgia that we could exhibit Shorthorn as an exclusive breed class. One of the many new shows organized at this time was the Piedmont Three County Show, consisting of Oconee, Morgan and Newton Counties in middle Georgia. As a Teacher of Agriculture, I met with the 4-H and FFA Advisors from each of the above counties to solicit their participation and secured Georgia Ag Farm Credit as the title sponsor of the event. The show rotated each year to one of the three counties, starting first at the Lions Club Fairgrounds in Madison, Georgia in 1985. The Georgia

Piedmont Show now consists of 15 counties of the Piedmont area of Georgia and has been in existence continuously for the past 30 years. It sure makes me feel good to have played a part in starting this livestock show that promotes youth and agriculture in our State.

At Oconee County High School as Vo-Ag Instructor and FFA Advisor for 22 years, we always had 10-20 Shorthorns each year in our show string. Every Spring we would hold an FFA Chapter Cattle Show for the student body on the football field. This school event was greatly looked forward to by our FFA members as an opportunity to compete against each other and improve their showmanship before going on to the regional show circuit.

One of the local shows that Oconee County FFA took part in was the Madison County Fair, located in Comer, Georgia. At one of the Madison County shows, we were unloading a young Shorthorn heifer and a passing car honked their horn and spooked the animal. She proved quite difficult to catch and stayed in a grove of trees behind the fairground for the duration of the fair. We would feed and water her everyday and by the end of the week she was ready to go home with the others. I remember telling my Vo-Ag classes that we have 22 head in the Madison county show and were keeping one in reserve, posted in the woods.

Another show that we consistently took 10-15 Shorthorn heifers to each year throughout the 1980s and 90s was the Augusta Exchange Club Show located in Augusta, Georgia, which is of course the home of the Masters Golf Tournament. Shorthorn cattle were not common in this area of the State and our big string of Shorthorns was a big attraction. The Club gave us great premiums in our own breed class. I was told the Augusta Exchange Club was one of the richest in the South.

At the Macon Fair show one year, the Angus, Hereford and Shorthorns (all British breeds) were shown against each other. Rodney Chandler from our FFA chapter had the British Breed Champion showing a registered Milking Shorthorn heifer.

Oconee FFA showed every year of the 22 years I was Vo-Ag. teacher at Oconee County at the Gwinnett County Southeastern Empire show located in Lawrenceville, Georgia near Atlanta. This was a very large show open to all States. One day at the lunch table in Oconee County High I was telling my fellow teachers what a great livestock facility they had in Gwinnett County. Our county school maintenance man said, "in 10 years, they won't have agriculture shows anymore because it will no longer be taught in schools." The football coach laughed and asked him, "are you ready to quit eating?"

Even though over the years of my teaching career we had shown several Champion and Reserve Champion Heifers and one year the State 'Best Group of Five' (all Shorthorn), many of my fellow Vo-Ag teachers told me you will never have a State Champion Steer that was a full blood Shorthorn. At the 1993 Junior National Livestock Show, David Mooney showed the Overall Champion: a Shorthorn. This steer's picture is placed on display with all winners since then at the Georgia Junior National Show Exhibit Hall located in Perry, Georgia.

1991 Georgia State "Best of Five" Heifers

One year in the 1970s, Hippies were prominent on Peachtree Street in Atlanta. We were showing our show string of Shorthorn heifers at the Southeastern Fairgrounds and some adults helping me were sleeping with our animals. Around midnight we were awakened by loud voices. It was the Atlanta police telling a group of Hippies that they could not be allowed to go through the livestock barn because the exhibitors washed their animals.

Those who told me I would never win a Georgia State show with a Shorthorn Steer had not seen the June 15, 1968 issue of the Shorthorn World. On page 13 of the issue is a picture of the Towns County FFA Chapter, back when only steer where shown in Georgia, with that year's Georgia State Reserve Champion. We had the Georgia State Reserve Champion in the 1960s three years in a row.

Charles Osborn was a 1969 Graduate of Oconee County High School who showed Shorthorn cattle and has maintained a Shorthorn herd since his graduation. In 2000, Charles wanted me to accompany him to the National Western Cattle Show held in Denver, Colorado.

He arranged for the airline tickets and we were excited about our trip. A short time before we were to leave, someone had hijacked a plane, so security was tight. The security personnel made Charles and I board the plane last both going and coming on our trip. We were also the only ones out of 150 passengers who were required to remove our shoes. Charles said it was the carryon bag I was carrying. I told Charles it was the suspicious grin he always wore on his face.

Georgia State Education did not allow girls to be in Vo-Ag. until 1970. That year, Paula Whitehead was my first female student. Paula wanted to show a steer. I took 6 students to Camella, Georgia on the Florida line to purchase 6 Shorthorn-Charolaise cross steers. We drew straws to see who would get which steer, because they all were good. Paula unfortunately drew the wildest calf. All these calves were around 500 pounds. Paula broke her calf to lead within 3 days by giving the animal constant attention and even sleeping with the calf in the barn. It took the 5 boys nearly 6 weeks to break their calves. I knew then, girls would be a great addition to Vo-Ag. programs in Georgia and my FFA Chapter. Mr. Jackson Jones, who was one of my adult farmers in Oconee County, had twin girls, Jackie and Jane Jones. He wanted to find two good Shorthorn heifers for them to show. Jackson placed a camper on the back of his pickup truck and we made a trip north to farms in Illinois and Indiana. One farm we stopped at was the Wise Farm in Bethamy, Illinois. The Wise family saw our car tag and were amused that it said, "Oconee" which was the name of their local county also. They pronounced the name different than us with, "Oak-a-knee" instead of our, "O-cone-E."

When Starling was 11 years old and Shannon was 9, my wife, Mary Ellen of 19 years died of Cancer. This was a great blow to all of us, for she was a wonderful wife and a loving mother. In my Vo-Ag. Program was the son of a recently deceased Agricultural Economics teacher at the University of Georgia. John Nixon and his wife Marilyn were from Mount Pilot, North Carolina, where John had taken Vo-Ag. in high school. Being influenced as I was by this experience, he completed a Doctorate degree from Michigan State with his young wife. A year before my wife passed away, John had also lost a battle with Cancer. Marilyn was left with a son David 16 and a daughter Melanie, 14. After a year of dating, we married and put our families together. We renamed our farm, 'K&M Shorthorns' and it has remained that till this day.

Georgia State Champion Shorthorn Heifer 1987 - Brennen Ward

The Bulls I have used of the last 50 years to improve my herd of Polled Shorthorns have been great and not so great. Listed below are the ones that I feel really helped me with herd improvement over the years. In the seventies and eighties, the Bulls I have already mentioned in this article certainly were great choices to improve any Shorthorn herd. Let me mention a few others that I am also happy we used in the K&M Polled herd.

Ridgecrest White Knight was a son of Ridgecrest Maria IV. He was a great white bull from a really good cow that we used in our herd heavily in the mid-80s. At the Waukaru Sale held September 14, 1991 we sought herd improvement cattle for the Jordan's family. A star must have been shining when we were able to secure Ridgecrest Maria IV "High Pockets" from the Ridgecrest Farms of Florida. At 13 years of age she started her transplant career. High Pockets was a magnificent cow that produced an outstanding offspring, even when bred to a poor-quality bull. Producing many outstanding heifers and Bulls for the Jordan family including a Champion pair of heifers and a Champion pair of Bulls at the 1989 Denver National Western Show. She was 17 years old when she died, having contributed not only to the United States history and genetics but even extending her remarkable impact across the globe. K&M Polled Shorthorns used her genetics heavily; that star also was shining for us. When Ridgecrest White Knight was sold at a local sale barn, many cattlemen asked, "where did you get that great Charolais bull?"

A great bull I mused throughout the 1990s was FS RB Irish Breeze, bred by Hodges Family Shorthorns of Oklahoma. He was sold in a Oklahoma Shorthorn sale and recommended to me by Mike Dugdale. Sired by HRS HL Red Baron (a bull I had seen at the North American) Red Baron was sired by Haze Leaf II; an Irish bull.

Starting in 1980 as a teacher of Agriculture and a Shorthorn breeder, I attended the North American International for 13 years consecutively. This was a show that I felt was a great help with my Shorthorn breeding program. It was also great each year to attend the Sutherland Sale at Louisville, Kentucky.

Another bull that left me with some top-quality females was LSF Milestone, sired by Deerpark Leader XIII, from a cow by Manalong Super Flag.

By attending the North American Expo, I had the opportunity to see bull like Rodeo Drive win the National Shorthorn Bull Championship. Later, I had an opportunity to purchase CCS Keystone, who was Rodeo Drive's full brother. He was bred in the Hoyt & Sons herd in Burns, Oregon. I purchased CCS Keystone from Mr. Bruce Wallace in East Bent, North Carolina on May 3, 1992. Keystone I thought had all the good qualities of Rodeo Drive, even having better structure, but he was a horned bull. However, when bred to good polled cows, I got very few horned calves and some great females for the K&M Polled Shorthorn herd.

Born in my herd, January 14, 1999 was a roan bull calf that I named Bridges Irish Shamrock. Sired by Tom's Bold who was sired by Philcon Cunia Dividend out of a 3W Payoff cow, which I purchased from Bruce Wallace. Many told me he was the best Shorthorn bull they had ever seen. The dam of Shamrock was sired by my FS RB Irish Breeze bull and out of a 5HP Milestone cow.

In 1998 the American Shorthorn Association started the WHR Registration System, which to date, I have been very pleased with. Being a member of the Jackson County (Georgia) Cattlemen's

Association, I served as President and started the Jackson County Purebred Breeder's Association. The Jackson County Cattlemen's Association submitted my name to the Georgia Cattlemen's Association and I was awarded the Georgia 1993 Purebred Breeder of the Year Award. I considered this a great honor being one of the very few Shorthorn breeders in Georgia, where there are many other breeders of many different breeds. My uncle, Guy Perry said it was my persistence with the Shorthorn breed that gained me the recognition. Calvin Coolridge said, "Press On! Nothing in the world can take the place of persistence. Talent will not; nothing is more common than unsuccessful men with talent. Genius will not:

unrewarded genius is almost a Proverb. Education alone will not; the world is full of educated derelicts. Persistence and determination alone are omnipotent."

The Georgia Farm Bureau Monitor (newspaper) made a short film documenting my award as Georgia Purebred Breeder of the Year for 1993. It was shown on public television, Bridges Irish Shamrock was filmed and included in the documentary.

I kept a Shorthorn sign out on US Highway 441. This highway is one which many Ohio cattlemen travel to Florida. Sam and Cindy Manful, with their daughter, Kristen stopped by our farm one year on their way back home. They purchased some Shorthorn females from our herd. Kristen was in the process of finishing high school and was showing cattle in their local shows. She sent me a picture of an AI sired bull calf that had been named Grand Champion bull, competing against 8 other breeds. Kristen named her bull "KW Kool Moose." Sending me a picture of the bull, she asked me if I would like to buy the animal. I really liked what I saw, so I told her yes. This was an outstanding March steer prospect and she was offered a high price for Kool Moose by many steer jockeys. KW Kool Moose came to the K&M Shorthorn farm on April 1, 2004.

After Kool Moose arrived at my farm, our newly formed Georgia Club Calf Producers website was established. I started selling a lot of Shorthorn heifers and steers to Alabama and Florida. Seeing Kool Moose calves win at the Georgia National Show in Perry, Georgia gave me great satisfaction. I began to have high demand from Georgia FFA and 4-H junior cattle show exhibitors.

On the Club Calf Award, points were given for winning or placing in six select Georgia State shows. The British breeds were classed together for point placing. Thomas Ross of Lumpkin County FFA placed 4th out of 69 calves in the 2010-11 Award ceremony.

I sent a copy of the 2010-2011 Georgia Club Calf Award Ceremony to our Executive Shorthorn Secretary, Mr. Bert L. Moore. Mr. Moore sent me back a letter stating in part, "Thank you for your letter and the awards ceremony brochure of the Georgia Club Calf Producers. Clearly is is an organization like this and people like you who provide much strength to youth programs and the Shorthorn breed. Being a source of stock and backing up purchases with success and assistance are important steps, not only in the development of junior members but also giving them the drive to become successful breeders of the Shorthorn breed."

Mr. E. J. Whitmire of Franklin, North Carolina that I previously mentioned was killed by a borrowed Charolais bull. This nearly happened to me on July 3, 2001. A Shorthorn 16-month-old bull attacked me in my holding pen as I was separating another young bull calf from the cow. It was my mistake, as I did not realize this cow was in heat and that this young bull had plans to breed her. God looked out for me as my 12-year-old granddaughter was with me and ran and got a neighbor to pull me from the holding pen. This was a very near-death experience, in fact my attending doctor told the nurses that I was crushed so bad he didn't think I would live. However, after a week in the Intensive Care and great care by my wife Marilyn and family, I lived to continue to breed Shorthorn cattle.

In my 50 years of breeding Shorthorns, my Shorthorn Bulls have been gentle and easy to manage. I learned a lesson that day. Also in 2005 I was diagnosed with Cancer and had my right kidney removed. I was lucky I did not need further treatments.

During 2001, my stepson David Nixon came back to the farm and became my farm manager. David has done a great job and played a large part in our farm winning the 2004 Purebred Breeder Award for the State of Georgia.

My son Starling Bridges, who is helping me put together my experiences breeding Shorthorns in Georgia for 50 years, had the opportunity to work with Dr. Stephen Dice, who was one of the very early animal scientists to have success in cloning beef cattle. I have a picture of Starling and a string of 5 cloned Angus calves. Also, over the past years Starling has spent many days on our farm helping me work our herd. Starling is a big part of some of our successes in breeding Shorthorn cattle. He is a graduate of UGA and now the director of a substance abuse treatment program in Helen, Georgia.

Earlier in my writing, I wrote that when Starling and Shannon were 3 and 6 years old they milked a cow called, 'Strawberry.' It was heart breaking to our family that on August 3, 2016 we lost Shannon to Cancer. Shannon was on the liver transplant list at Emory Hospital in Atlanta but developed Stomach Cancer and did not survive the treatments. Her brother Starling you see in our Shorthorn cow-milking picture with Shannon worked hard transporting his sister back and forth to Atlanta to treatments for several months. On one trip, Shannon asked Starling, "If this doesn't work out, will you speak at my funeral?"

Starling wrote and delivered her Eulogy at the memorial service where over 1100 people attended, after over 2000 people came to the family visitation the night before. Many called his Eulogy a masterpiece; the best they had ever read or ever heard. Here I want to quote Starling from the Eulogy he gave that referenced Shannon's love of animals, including the polled Shorthorns she was raised with:

> *"Shannon heard the teachings of Christ where in John 13, verse 34 he tells us: "Love one another. As I have loved you, you should love* **One Another**.*"*
>
> *Shannon and I were blessed to be raised on a farm with many animals and since we were all created by God, my sister saw the animals as* **"One Anothers."** *If one of dad's hunting dogs had puppies, you could always find Shannon in the kennels with the momma dog, loving on the puppies. If you brought a baby to our house, Shannon would stay near the child and help any way she could, because babies were even better than puppies."*

Shannon's 47 years of life was an example of how we as humans should live; we should love one another and take good care of the livestock God places on our care.

I have in my possession a copy of George Smith's "*All in a Lifetime,*" written by a prominent South Carolina Shorthorn breeder. I got to know Dr. Smith who helped organize the Southeastern Shorthorn Association. Also, he held many Junior Shorthorn Field Day events and four of the Southeastern Shorthorn Field Days. I had an opportunity to judge some of his Junior Field Day Shorthorn Heifer Shows. Dr. Smith taught Vocational Agriculture in Georgia for 12 years. Then he went to Ohio State University, where he obtained his Veterinary Degree and eventually setting up his veterinary practice in Mauldin, South Carolina. Dr. Smith in his book tells of many large animal vet experiences. All though he treated many small animals in his practice, he would always treat large farm animals whenever the need arose. I found I could easily get a local vet to come do bi-annual inoculations and other services in the 1960s, 70s and 80s but that became difficult in the 1990s. Oconee County High School was located 5 miles away from the UGA Vet School a and I had no problem getting them to come treat our FFA Chapter Club Calves. They would bring vet students who were in training to work with large animals. I am also blessed to be on their herd health program and this gives the UGA Vet School the chance to bringing training students to my farm in the present day. Georgia has a serious problem in vets needed to treat cattle, so much so that the Georgia Department of Agriculture is starting a program that will help a vet student pay off their education loans if they will agree to treat large animals on Georgia farms for a set time period. The Georgia Department of Education had the same program years back with there was a severe shortage of Vocational Agriculture teachers in Georgia.

I had many enjoyable experiences going to Southeastern Field Days. One field day memory was at an event held at Mr. Roy Dedmon's farm in Shelby, NC. We had a bad Army Worm infestation that year in Georgia. Roy ask me at the field day, "do you have any

Army Worms?" I ask him, "How many do you want?" My first experience with Army Worms was when I was a teacher in Hiawassee, GA. Mr. Reuben Walls, a Shorthorn breeder previously mentioned had 10 acres of prime fescue grass he was going to cut for hay. On Friday of that week he called me excited, "you have got to come see this!" Army Worms had eaten both 5-acre fields to the ground. A paved highway ran between the two fields and the road had to be closed because of the slick hazard caused by millions of worms moving from one field to the next. It was definitely one of the most amazing experiences in my 50 years of breeding Shorthorns. Starting in 1966 as a new Shorthorn breeder, I made it a point to visit and get to know as many Southeastern Shorthorn breeders as possible. Being a Vo. Ag. teacher, I also took as many of my students to these visits as I could.

My Shorthorn World, August 15, 1968 issue listed 7 Georgia breeders, 3 Florida breeders, 3 Tennessee breeders, 3 South Carolina breeders and 6 North Carolina breeders. I would like to list my fine experiences getting to know these breeders and thank them for helping me get off to a good start as a Shorthorn cattle breeder. I also know there were many other breeders in the Southern states that did not list an ad in the magazine, some that really helped me and I've already mentioned.

In Georgia, I got to know Mr. Gaynor and Emory Shurley of Warrenton, Georgia. These brothers were using the bull Lynwood Quest. Over several years they gave me good advice on how to select good, balanced Shorthorns. It was always a blessing to visit their farm.

In South Carolina, the Pine Lane farm of Mr. Jack Dobbins Townville had a very outstanding herd from which I purchased several winning heifers for my FFA students. Mr. T. Elias McGee at Starr, SC had a great Shorthorn herd of over 200 cows. Mr. McGee used the bull Sutherland Banker, Louada Crofter. At the Tennessee National Sale, Mr. McGee was in attendance and purchased two very good bulls. It was later than Mr. McGee introduced me his kinfolks; Mr. Ned McGill and his wife Willene. In the Ned McGill family was a son named Steve. As many of you know, after completing a degree at LSU, Steve McGill worked several years with the American Shorthorn Association as the Youth Activities Director. Just this year, I helped on of our local farmers purchase a great young polled Shorthorn bull from South Starr Farm in Iva, SC. The Ned McGill/Steve McGill family are good people to know if you are raising quality Shorthorns.   In planning our Southeastern Shorthorn Spring Sale, on Sunday afternoons we would meet at the home of Randy and Nancy Griffis' home in central South Carolina to plan the sale and the Junior Shorthorn Show, which was held each year at the Carolina Junior Beef Roundup. As the Young Farmer teacher here in Jackson County Georgia, I took FFA students with Shorthorn projects to the Carolina Junior Beef Roundup held the first weekend of August. One of the students I took was Shawn Collins, who now is a Vo. Ag. Teacher in Moultrie, Georgia. Shawn is doing a great job with his own Shorthorn herd and his FFA students have shown several State Shorthorn Heifer Champions. Shawn while in high school was my K&M Shorthorn herdsman. With Shawn's help we kept the K&M Shorthorn herd in top shape.

In my July 1994 Shorthorn Country magazine on page 46, Bruce Wallace, the owner of Flint Hill Farms in East Bend, NC states, "It all started in 1940 with a blue-ribbon steer at the 1940 South Dakota State Fair, where the animal brought $.16/pound." The Flint Hill Farm established by Bruce and Sandra Wallace became a place that for many years I could buy affordable Shorthorn cattle for myself and my students. It was a great pleasure for me to look through his 200+ herd of registered Shorthorns that he had purchased from all over the United States and Canada. Bulls he was using at that time were: 'GS Payback PO89,' 'C Pancho SE 549,' 'Mr. Syndicator,' 'GEG Golden Doc 405th,' '35H Maverickx. Bruce states in his ad, "Herd Dispersion, June 5, 2020, 1:00 pm at the farm." My Pastor, the Rev. Larry Davidson of Bogart, Georgia, who Bruce helped get his sons polled Shorthorn heifers and start a Davidson Shorthorn herd took part in his memorial service. Mr. Bruce Wallace and his wife Sandra's Shorthorn herd was dispersed after his death. My brother Thomas who I helped develop his Shorthorn herd attended this sale and purchased some fine Shorthorn cattle. As Shorthorn sales go, "The Lewisfield Complete Shorthorn Dispersion" advertised in the February 1, 1967 Shorthorn World as, "The Largest Sale of the Century" held February 25, 1967 at Charlottesville, VA was a sale that for some reason I missed. In the sale catalog there are 206 individual cattle listed with their full pedigrees for both Dam and Sire listed for 2 generations of each animal. There are also big pictures for a lot of herd bulls, cows, calves and bulls like 'Shirgarton Ranger' imported from Scotland and 'Roan Lad' of Northwood, by Clipper King of Bapton, a 2,670-pound imported bull. I have heard it said, "Nothing beats a great set of

Leggs." One of my students that I taught in Vo. Ag. at Oconee high school got me to go with him on trips throughout the United States to see Shorthorn cattle. On one if these trips, we saw 'WO Divident 3J (Leggs)' that was 'Len Ru TA Leaders full brother. The young man name is Shell Ward and his mother said I 'overdone' her son when I introduced him to Shorthorn Cattle.

One time I had a minister of one of our local churches call me, telling me he had a large group of young people from China who wanted to visit a cattle farm. I told him I would be glad to show them my Shorthorn herd. I soon learned from the questions they asked that they had little knowledge of cattle. They wanted to know what I did with my cows when it rains. It was very worth my time to introduce them to how a United States cattle farm was run. I enjoyed their visit.

There is a creek that runs through my farm. This creek has served as a good source of water for my herd for many years. Problems began in the 1990s when a large woodmill was built two miles upstream. the Georgia Environmental Protection Agency gave them a permit to dump waste water from the plant into the creek. Tannic acid from the pine bark started causing us to have calves born with deformities. The UGA Vet Lab tested the water and did autopsies on the deformed calves to determine the tannic acid was causing liver damage that led to the deformed calves. The creek lost fish and wildlife, becoming a dead creek with high concentrations of bacteria.

To eliminate my new problem with water supply, we fenced out the creek and drilled an expensive, deep well. My wife Marilyn and I visited the driller at the site under construction and asked how things are going. "Not well I'm afraid," he said. "I'm down now 400 fcct and only getting 3 gallons a minute." My wife was quite worried and decided we needed to pray right then and there for God to provide. By the time she finished praying, water was shooting high into the air at a rate of over 100 gallons a minute. This was enough water to supply a small town. The water tested excellent in every way and solved my deformed calf problems.

No one can tell me God has not helped me many times in my Vo. Ag. school teaching and my registered Shorthorn cattle. One example where he helped me was after I retired from teaching. I took a part-time job at the local county detention center, that had a farm operation that was run by the inmates. They grew different types of plants in a greenhouse and has a small cattle operation. One day in the greenhouse while working with the inmates, I had a dried gourd with a round hole in it that a Martin bird could use as a house. I placed the gourd on a table and out came a large spider. I tapped the gourd on the table and the spider returned to the gourd. Carefully I put the gourd back on the shelf where I found it. A few days later, some grammar school teachers brought some first/second grade students on a field trip to the farm to learn about plants. This was around the time the movie, 'Charlotte's Web' was showing in theatres. I remembered the gourd and asked the students if they'd like to meet Charlotte from the movie. Their eyes grew big as they all said yes. I reached for the gourd up on the shelf, tapped it on the table and out came the spider. I told the kids to say 'hello' to Charlotte! I tapped the gourd on the table and the spider returned to its home. I put the gourd back on the shelf, as the children stood there in wonder. Also, in the greenhouse we had a beautiful Gardenia bush in full bloom. I told everyone to get in line and they could now smell the world's greatest-smelling flower. None of them told me afterwards they did not think the Gardenia was the World's greatest smelling flower.

On January 22, 2017, I attended the Piedmont Junior Cattle Show. This was a show I helped organize as a rotating 3 county junior show in our area. At this show, I was awarded a beautiful plaque as appreciation for getting this show started and supporting it for over 40 years. It now includes 16 counties. There were 148 head of cattle in the show this year, making it one of Georgia's largest shows. The current show committee told me they had raised over $8000.00 to use as awards for Junior members participating in the Piedmont Show. At last year's show, I met a 2-year-old girl named Presleigh Smith. As I sat in the stands watching the show beside her mother and great aunt, Presleigh let me hold her just like I was her dad even though she did not know me. I was very impressed with Presleigh. At this year's show, I saw the little girl again and I heard her tell her grandmother she wanted a show stick just like her cousin Hunter Spear had, and she wanted it pink. I had in my cattle barn a small show stick, and I had been wondering for a long time what I was going to ever do with it. Now I knew that God introduced me to Presleigh so I would know right where that stick needed to go. A close friend of mine, Vickie McElroy, who also knew Presleigh, told me she would paint the show stick pink and presented to Presleigh as a gift from me. I told Vickie that maybe God would let me live long enough to see Presleigh use that show stick in a Junior Show. Her cousin, Hunter Spear is a 10th Grade student at Commerce High School who I am also deeply impressed with. He has told me he wants to become a teacher of Agriculture. I have told his parents that I plan to do all I can to help Hunter fulfill this dream. Hunter and his family live in the city of Commerce. Georgia. He was given the chance to work at a local livestock farm and like me, also given the chance to show a calf in the local Junior Cattle Show circuit. Hunter also helps the owner of the farm, Marty Seagraves with his own children's show cattle, which show extensively. The Seagraves family hold every Summer for high school, middle school and even grammar school children what they call a Livestock Boot Camp. If you could see the Seagraves introducing all the children to livestock at this camp it would surely warm your heart. I certainly did mine. Hunter was assigned the teaching job at the Boot Camp relating to beef cattle and the care of them. Teaching how to halter break, feed, groom and show a club calf is just some of the things he instructs the children.

I took time off from my hay work to attend a day at the boot camp last summer. There I saw Hunter do an outstanding job of teaching the cattle work I listed above. It seems that after seeing and hearing Hunter perform as a teacher to children, there is no doubt in my mind that, if given the chance, he will become an excellent Teacher of Agriculture. Hunter's grandmother, Vickie McElroy tells me that Presleigh will be attending this year's Livestock Boot Camp. I am so very happy that God let me give her a pink show stick.

In checking my Shorthorn Country, January 2007 issue, I find the results of the Naile Shorthorn Steer Futurity and Breeders Cup Steer Show. The Champion Purebred and Champion Breeders Cup in the 'on foot' show was exhibited by Austin Hanson. The steer was also the Reserve Champion Carcass Steer. He was sired by *AR SU Lu Kool 1007. KU Koel Moose* has also sired some top Georgia steers and like to mention was some pictures of some of them. Kellie Keener of Toccoa, Georgia in March 2013 purchased from K&M Shorthorn a red and white steer calf. The price I sold it to her for was $1000.00. Kellie's steer was born December 2012, which would make him a lightweight steer when shown during the summer of 2013. Her steer was Champion over all in several shows including her county show. At the Georgia State Steer Show, he weighed 1050 pounds. The word had gotten around what a great finish show steer he would be. Kellie sold the steer and he left Georgia for Iowa.

Another trip made by Shell Ward and I in the late 1990s was to Texas to attend the Texas Belt Buckle Bonanza. At this event, we were introduced to a new wrinkle in steer showing. They were classifying the steers by breed. you could have a red Shorthorn with papers, but if they one classifying the animals decided it was a red Angus, that's who you ended up in the ring with. They were using so called 'breed experts' from other States to place the steers in the proper classes. Shell and I learned a lot about what was about to come to the Georgia State Show. Two years later, using cattle experts from Texas, we started classifying Georgia steers by breed in our state show. One of my students entered his Shorthorn steer in our Atlanta show.

Kellie Keener and her award winning steer in 2013

A steer that had been entered on paper as a Red Angus, was changed
to a Shorthorn for the Atlanta show. This same red steer with a white
spot on his forehead was entered into the fall show as a Hereford.
Entered first as a Red Angus, then won the show as a Shorthorn, and
then won the fall show as a Hereford. I might add that it was one of
our State officials (who was in charge of setting up the shows)
daughter who owned the red steer. In 2017, there is a push to turn
most of our breeds black and no need to classify steers. I never though
I see a full registered Black Hereford, but there was one in the
Hereford show two weeks ago.

Ms. Caroline Waldrop, a FFA high school student at Forsyth County High showed an outstanding steer from K&M Shorthorns throughout Georgia, which won many shows. Her father is a Teacher of Agriculture.

Caroline Waldrop's 2015 Shorthorn Steer State Champion

Mr. Thomas Ross of Lumpkin County FFA started purchasing show heifers from K&M Shorthorns as a freshman in high school. One year, Purina Feed Company sponsored a show for juniors at Calhoun, Georgia. They put all breeds together, weighed them and place them in class by weight. There was a total of 77 heifers. Thomas won his class and then his heifer was picked as the third best female of the

Purina Show. Thomas won many shows with K&M Shorthorn heifers throughout his high school FFA career. The Ross' now have a very good Shorthorn herd of their own.

At the 2000 Georgia National Fair Open Show, Taylor Schiezer exhibited the Champion Shorthorn heifer, which was purchased from K&M Shorthorns. Taylor's grandfather, Darrell Seagraves is part of the Livestock Boot Camp I mentioned earlier. This show was a very competitive event with Shorthorn breeders from several States exhibiting animals.

Taylor Schieszer with the 2009 Georgia State Champion Shorthorn Heifer

A steer purchased by Marina Morgan of Franklin, North Carolina was shown throughout that State winning Shorthorn and overall Grand Champion awards. This steer was sired by Bridges Shamrock.

Back in 2012, Eli Smallwood from Monticello, Georgia purchased two Shorthorn heifers from K&M Shorthorns, a roan January calf and a roan March calf. I let him pay $800.00 for each of the calves, with $400.00 down and the remaining to be paid when the heifers were picked up in the summer. Starting with these two heifers, Eli now has a very good Shorthorn herd. With the help of his family, Eli has added some good heifers from the Bill and Beckey Rasor Farm located in Texas. Eli Smallwood is now the Georgia Junior Cattlemen

Association's Chapter Relations Officer. In the Georgia Cattlemen December 2016 issue, Eli writes an article. The story tells that his love of cattle came on Christmas when his uncle gave him his first calf. Since that first gifted animal, he has grown his own registered herd of Shorthorns. Eli Smallwood is a high school senior this year and has a bright future. I have just attended this year's Georgia National Junior Cattle Show where Eli exhibited the Champion Shorthorn Heifer. One of the two heifers I sold Eli in 2012 was the 2013 Georgia National Junior Livestock Show Reserve Champion Shorthorn Heifer.

Eli Smallwood with the 2013 Shorthorn Reserve Champion Heifer

Located three miles from my farm is a 500-acre Shorthorn cattle and chicken farm. Beginning around the late 1950s began to build for the Jesse Jewell Processing Plant in Gainesville, Georgia that processed broilers. Cotton farms during that time began to change to cattle farms and the chicken litter from the broiler operations was excellent fertilizer for the worn-out red soil. It is a complete fertilizer plus it contains organic matter that helps with erosion. Within the last 20 years, over 20 new poultry operations have come to Georgia.

Tripp Rogers operates the cattle/chicken farm near me called Calamit Farms. It has a herd of about 150 brood cows. He started with a mixture of breeds but no Shorthorns. His cattle became very hard to manage. I introduced the Shorthorn breed to Tripp, who purchased several Shorthorn bulls from me over the last 15 years. This introduction of the Shorthorn bloodline has calmed down his herd and increased milk supply for his calves. Tripp has also purchased some registered Shorthorns from me and from the Manful's of Ohio. Tripp and his wife Faith have two daughters; Audrey and Sarah. While they were FFA members at East Jackson High School, they both showed Shorthorn heifers at the Georgia National Show in 2001. Both girls did a great job and their heifers placed high in the show.

Audrey Rogers 2001 Georgia National Show

Sara Rogers 2001 Georgia National Show

I received a call just before Christmas of 2011 from Marcus and Monia Turner of Box Springs, Georgia. Their son Justin was entering the 9th grade and taking Vo. Ag. at Box Springs High School. Justin wanted for his Christmas present a show heifer, FFA Club Calf. I explained to Justin's parents that I had an excellent Shorthorn Plus heifer born in September and that it would be ready to wean around February 1, 2012. They came and took a picture of this calf and placed the photo under the Christmas tree. I sold this Shorthorn Plus calf to them for $800.00. I had also offered this calf to another student, now a senior that have previously purchased winning Shorthorn heifers from me. Being his senior year, he wanted to really win big, so he went to Iowa instead and purchased a Shorthorn Plus calf for $5000.00. His calf was born also in September of 2011, so the two calves showed in the same class in the 2012 Club Calf shows. Justin with his $800.00 K&M Shorthorn calf beat the $5000.00 calf 3 places in 3 different State shows. At the 2013 Georgia National Jr. Livestock Show, Justin's calf placed 3rd in a class of 16 Shorthorn Plus calves. Justin also came back in 2013-14 and purchased 2 more registered Shorthorn heifers and a bull. Now this year (2017), Justin is a senior in high school. He is President of his FFA Chapter, graduating as an honor student and making college plans to major in Agriculture. I might add that he has plans to expand his Shorthorn herd he has started in high school.

While attending the 2017 Georgia State Jr. Cattle Show, I was approached by Miss Ashley Sapp of Bloomingdale, Georgia. This show is held in Perry, Georgia in February of each year. Ashley sat down with me at this show to tell me, "Mr. Bridges, I want you to know that I am now teaching Agriculture at my local middle school." Ashley called me in the Spring of 2011. She had been showing goats in her local FFA shows and she had seen my Shorthorn Club Calf heifers at the State show and she wanted to purchase one. On March 4, 2011, Ashley's parents, Richie and Sheryl, brought Ashley to our farm and bought a red/white heifer for $1000.00. I named this heifer, *Bridges Bella Brooke.* I chose this name for a little girl named Bella Brooke who was the daughter of friends of mine, Rodney and Gay Chandler. Bella Brooke had started showing cattle at age 8 and was doing a super job with her show calf. Her father Rodney Chandler had also shown calves from our farm. At the 2012 Georgia State Jr. Livestock Show, I had the pleasure of introducing little Bella Brooke to Ashley Sapp and the calf named after her. Both Ashley and Bella Brooke seemed very pleased.

Ashley Sapp and Bridges Bella Brooke

Also, later in May of 2012, we held our Spring Club Calf Awards Program, which is tallied from points turned in by exhibitors, from their showing in the 6 State Club Calf shows. It was a pleasure to take a picture with Ashley as she received the top Club Calf award for that year. The lady that is seen in the background of this picture (seated) is Jane Farmer, the grandmother of Bella Brooke Chandler. Ashley attended the University of Georgia on a music scholarship and played trumpet in the Georgia Red Coat Band.

Ashley Sapp and Kenneth Bridges, 2012 Georgia Club Calf Awards Program

The Georgia Shorthorn Association was organized as a State association in the early 1980s. For several years, it was a strong association. One of the Georgia Shorthorn Association's activities was to have different members set up a Shorthorn Exhibit Booth in their local County fair with Shorthorn promotional material obtained from the American Shorthorn Association. Also, members of the Georgia Shorthorn Association passed out material at Georgia Cattlemen's Association events. In an effort to increase Shorthorn Junior Cattle Show numbers and to increase the number of commercial cattlemen using Shorthorn bulls, the Association started a Junior Awards program for our State Show. We were honored to have two Southeastern Shorthorn breeders join us in this award. Flint Hill Farm, owned by Bruce Wallace in East Bend, North Carolina and Garvin Creek Cattle Company owned by Randy and Nancy Griffis from central, South Carolina.

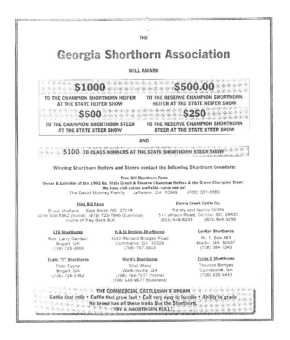

An example of two students who took advantage of our State Association Awards program were Laura and Kristy Smith of the Madison County 4-H Club. Their mom brought them to our farm the Summer of 1997. They purchased a white heifer and a red heifer. Both Laura and Kristi did well in the Georgia show circuit. Kristi, showing the red heifer at several 4-H, FFA Junior shows had the Champion Heifer, including the 1998 Reserve Champion Shorthorn Heifer. This animal was sired by *Rodeo Drive's* full brother, *Keystone*.

The white heifer was later bred to *Tom's Bold,* a *Phil Con Cunia Dividend* son. The result of this mating on January 14, 1999 was *Bridges Irish Shamrock.* At the 1999 Georgia National Livestock Show, the Smith girls won the Shorthorn Cow/Calf Class with the white cow and *Bridges Irish Shamrock* at her side.

Picture Perfect
Photo

    It really pleases me that Kristi now has an 8-year-old son named Allan, showing Shorthorn heifers. A former student of mine from Oconee County, (also still a Shorthorn breeder) Charles Osborn is sponsoring Allan a Shorthorn heifer to show.

    It also pleases me that I had the opportunity to teach Katie Osborn, Charles and Vickie Osborn's daughter when she was an 8th grade student of mine at Oconee County High School. Katie was an outstanding young lady, the kind any teacher of Vocational Agriculture would like to have in their classroom. Katie showed Shorthorn heifers throughout high school. She had the class winner in a large, strong class of Shorthorn heifers at the 1996 Georgia National Livestock Show in Perry, Georgia.

Also, at the 1997 Georgia National she exhibited another class winner. Both heifers were sired by *Keystone*.

In the May/June 2010 Shorthorn Country magazine, the front cover is a picture of a young girl holding a show stick. She is Alexis Koelling from Herman, Montana. She is getting a little advice from the judge at the National Western show. This picture taken by Cindy Cagwin Johnston is a great example that Shorthorn cattle and kids go hand-in-hand. Presleigh Smith, the little girl that I presented a show stick to will get this copy of my Shorthorn Country magazine. The issue also has some beautiful pictures of Shorthorn cattle. I bet Presleigh Smith will call this her, 'Cow Book.'

The year was 1990 and I had just completed 30 years of teaching Agricultural Education in Georgia high schools. In Georgia, that much teaching is enough for full retirement pay. I had taught 5 years at Union County High School at Blairsville, 3 years at Towns County High in Hiawassee and 22 years at Oconee County High School in Watkinsville, Georgia. Knowing I was considering retirement, I was contacted by Mrs. Janet Adams, the Vocational Supervisor for Jackson County High School. Mrs. Adams and the Vo. Ag. Teachers at the high school wanted to start a full time Young Farmers program for Jackson County. They felt that I would be an excellent choice to get the program established. Since K&M Shorthorns is located in Jackson County, I told them I would be glad to spend two years getting the program up and running. I was to start work on July 1, 1990 and my wife Marilyn, knowing I was going to retire in June ask me to take her to bible conference at Stonecroft Ministries being held in Branson, Missouri in late June of that year. Marilyn had started a Stonecroft Bible Study group in Athens, Georgia

20 years before. She had always wanted to go to their headquarters. Mrs. Adams told me to go to the conference in Missouri, and then I could start the Young Farmer's program.

In taking Marilyn to Missouri, it allowed me to visit Merl and Eileen Welch at Green Ridge Shorthorns. In my October 1990 *Shorthorn Country* issue on page 3, Merl and Eileen Welch give a picture of their grandchildren; Blake, Carly, Alex and Welch. Also on page 5 of this issue are some of their great Shorthorn calves consigned to sale at Urbana, Missouri on December 8, 1990. On page 8/9, Waukaru introduces sires *Spry's Stars and Stripes VI ET* and their selling semen rights on Waukaru's *Prime Minister ET*, whose dam is Waukaru's *Prima Donna*. She traces back to the great Shorthorn cow *Ridgecrest Maria II*, affectionately called "High Pockets." These are Shorthorn genetics that I have greatly used in my K&M Shorthorn program.

In the Bible in Genesis chapter 3, verse 18 it says, *And to Adam, God said, "Because you listened to your wife and ate the fruit when I told you not to, I have placed a curse upon the soil. All your life you will struggle to extract a living from it. It will grow thorns and thistles."* I had no thistles on my K&M Shorthorn Farm until about 1985. By 1990, with fertilizing with chicken manure, thistles had become a problem in Northeast Georgia. David Coker and his wife Geraldine came to my farm from Blairsville, Georgia to buy two polled Shorthorn bulls. They commented that they saw I had thistles like they did. I told them the Bible tells me I would have thistles. About the time, my 5-year-old granddaughter Garnette Smith was told the story of Adam and Eve in Sunday School. One day while driving across the pasture and seeing the thistle she said, "Grandpa, I hate what Adam and Eve went and did to us."

With thistle being a major cattle pasture problem, our local Jackson County Extension Agent was introducing a bug called the 'thistle weevil' that he said he was getting from the State of Missouri. I was able to make a trip from Branson, Missouri up to Urbana, Missouri and visit the Welch's at Green Ridge Shorthorns when I took my wife to Stonecroft Ministries. To my surprise, Merl told me he had never heard of a 'thistle weevil.' The only way I am controlling thistle in my pasture today is by spraying herbicide. I still have thistle on my K&M Shorthorn Farm. Thanks Adam.

Marilyn and I had a great trip to Missouri. She enjoyed her Stonecroft Ministries headquarters and I was greatly impressed with the Green Ridge Program.

As I mentioned earlier in my experiences with raising Shorthorns in Georgia, I learned how to AI breed my student's show heifers to keep down cost. On the back cover of the *Shorthorn Country Herd Reference Issue* of July 1985 is a listing of AI bulls offered by Time Share Breeding Service from Elk Grove, California. Mr. Tom James, their Genetics Coordinator was raised in the small South Georgia town of Adrian. He was very helpful with my ordering bull semen from Timeshare Breeding Services. He told me that his Grandfather's name was carved into the concrete sidewalk of Adrian, Georgia. We would travel through Adrian many times delivering Shorthorn cattle to customers in the South Georgia area.

From Time Share we purchased *RPS Tribune 82*, who was sired by *Mollie's Defender Adair*. *RPS Tribune 82* is the sire of *Rodeo Drive* and my herd sire *CCS Keystone 82*. Other sires purchased were: *Ramson 2416, Goliath* and *Instant Replay*. Tom James told me Time Share Breeders was importing a horn Shorthorn bull to produce steers named *Deer Park Improver 57*.

It seems I keep referring to *Keystone* so at this point let me show you a picture of him and some of the fine show cattle he sired for K&M Shorthorns.

CCS Keystone 82

Beth Armour of Olgelthorpe FFA purchased some Keystone heifers from me. Here is a picture of one of Keystone's daughters who won Champion Shorthorn Heifer at a very competitive Ag. Georgia Farm Credit Show. All during high school Beth Armour did a great job with her Shorthorn heifers.

At a large four county show at Tifton, Georgia in February of 1993, Jerry Wehunt of Sycamore, Georgia exhibited the Supreme Champion over all breeds with a K&M Shorthorn heifer.

As I mentioned my Georgia Club Calf website, K&M Shorthorns has sold club calves to 4-H and FFA members in Florida. Back in 2006, Diane Rodriguez of Okeechobee, Florida purchased a show steer from us. This steer did well in the Florida State Steer Show. At the time Diane purchased her steer she was a senior in high school, thus ending her FFA livestock career. However, she sent me a nice letter of appreciation for my help in her Shorthorn steer project. Diana also sent me a photo of the K&M Shorthorn steer:

Diane Rodriguez - Okeechobee, FL

Another Florida customer, Alexa Wandrey who is the mother of Heather Wandrey wrote me a nice letter saying:

"My daughter purchased a Shorthorn heifer from you in 2013 (Bridges Sadie Brooke). The heifer did excellent for my daughter and has now produced 2 great bull calves. The first one was my daughter's market steer for this last year's county fair. He finished 2nd in his weight class but was awarded Grand Champion Carcass. Her second calf, who she will be showing for this upcoming year, is a little powerhouse and he has already done great things in his first two shows this season at 7 months old. Sadie Brooke has been an awesome cow. She has calved amazing and unassisted and of course been an excellent mother. We love her and she is now bred again and

we are expecting another calf in September (hoping for a Shorthorn heifer). Do you have any Spring heifers? Let me know if you have one available. We want one!"

I checked my records. Alexa Wandrey's heifer was sired by *KW Kool Moose* and the dame being *K&M North Star*. North Star is still in my herd, turning out great calves each year.

Mrs. Elizabeth Coggins of Roopville, Georgia purchased a North Star's heifer from us last year; a great roan heifer that she plans to show this year in the open Shorthorn shows.

On April 10th of this year (2017), I received a letter from Mr. Ben Lastly, the Executive Secretary of the Georgia FFA Association. Mr. Lastly stated in his letter to me that Georgia now has over 41,000 FFA members across the State. He told me Georgia is now the 3rd largest State membership in the Nation. He wrote that at this year's 89th Georgia FFA Convention, he wanted me to join him on stage in recognition of the 100th Anniversary of the Smith-Hughes Act of 1917. The Smith-Hughes Act made Vocational Agriculture a subject taught in our Nation's school systems.

A short time later, Georgia State Vice President, Ms. Sadie Lackey came by my home, spent two hours with me to get my story of going from a County FFA Officer to a Teacher of Agriculture and an FFA Advisor. On stage, I was set before 5000 FFA delegates from all 159 counties. Ms. Lackey did an outstanding job telling how I was impacted by the Smith-Hughes Act as a high school student and also my record as a Teacher of Agriculture for 41 years in Georgia. She told of the many students of Vo. Ag. FFA that I had the privilege of teaching, and how my story was a direct result of the Smith-Hughes Act. I was told that I had a solemn look on stage that night. They could not see the tears I shed, as this was the most humbling experience of my lifetime. I cannot remember when people before came up to me, asking to have their picture taken with me. One wanting a picture was a Ms. Abbey Gretsch of Lexington, Georgia, who became a National FFA Vice President in 2016. The first Christian school to have Vo. Ag. in Georgia was the school Abbey attended. In 2012, a former student of mine from Oconee High School came to see me, telling me he was sending his daughter to Athens Christian School. He wanted her to have the same experience he had as a Vo. Ag. FFA student. His name was David Whitehead and he asked me to help him get a Vo. Ag. Program started at her school. A year later, Abby Gretsch enrolled in Athens Christian and had the opportunity to be a Vo. Ag. Student. As stated before, she eventually went on to be elected National FFA Vice President and travel across the Nation representing the National FFA organization. Abbey wanted her picture taken with me.

As a teacher, I would show my students the films on "The Four Star Farmers of America." I would tell them that Oconee County FFA might one day have a FFA Four Star Farmer. The students didn't believe me, as Oconee County was one of the smallest in Georgia. Then there was Andy and Charles Hillsman enrolled in my Vo. Ag. classes, who showed a string of Shorthorn and Beefmaster heifers and steers all four years they were students of Vo. Ag. at Oconee County

High School. Charles was elected State FFA Vice President in his senior year and all through high school kept great records of his Vo. Ag. Projects. Andy went off to college, but Charles stayed on the farm building his cattle farm operation. In 1981, I entered Charles Hillsman into the running for the Four Star Farmer of America Award. He was chosen as the Southern States FFA Star Farmer, and runner-up FFA Star Farmer of America for that year. I had always told my Oconee County Vo. Ag. students that the FFA Star Farmer of America had to come from somewhere, why not Oconee County? Charles Hillsman proved that I could be right. Now in 2017, Charles has a great farming operation. He included Shorthorn cattle in his success.

This year's State FFA Convention awards reminded me of the one above and many others my FFA students won over the years. I was also privileged to see current students I have worked with in building their Shorthorn operations be recognized. One was Eli Smallwood (page 57) who was chosen Georgia FFA Star Farmer and placed 2nd in the Beef Proficiency Award. He also exhibited the State Champion Shorthorn Heifer this year. Justin Turner (page 50) was awarded 2nd place in the State Electrical Wiring Award and showed the State Reserve Champion Shorthorn Heifer. As the Shorthorn breeder that started them off, it was a great pleasure for me to see them successful.

While teaching Vo. Ag. FFA in Oconee County, I had in my classes two brothers; Brad and Brian Shelnutt. They started showing Shorthorn heifers with our FFA Show Team. Their parents, Buddy and Kathy Shelnutt really got interested in their son's Shorthorn heifer projects, and this led to them starting a registered Shorthorn herd on their farm in Bishop, Georgia. Buddy and Kathy started purchasing Shorthorns from sales throughout the United States. They started attending the Shorthorn shows in the 1990s at the North American, held in Louisville, Kentucky every year. Kathy became very interested in the Shorthorn Lassie organization, a women's auxiliary of the American Shorthorn Association. She volunteered her services and became a member of the National Shorthorn Lassie Board from 1996 to 2000. In 2000, she served as president. Kathy Shelnutt tells me that she really enjoyed working with the Lassie Board members. I took the time to read page 70 *'Meet the Board'* in the Tartan Plaid, their publication. It is good to know the Lassie Board write up in my March 2017 issue of *Shorthorn Country* has great women to carry on the many activities of the Tartan Plaid.

In checking my copy of the May 2000 *Shorthorn Country,* it brings back the memories of two pleasant experiences. The Livestock Expo Exhibition located at Perry, Georgia has to be one of America's best. On page 26 is the write up of the Georgia National Livestock Shorthorn Show. I was involved in this show as a Georgia Shorthorn breeder. The judge for the show was Doug Parrott. He chose the Champion Bull to be *PBF Royal Trump* from Point Breeze Farm out of New Waterford, Ohio. The Champion Female was *CV Lucky Charm Co 29* from Caney Valley Farm in Lakeland, Florida. 'Pair of Females,' 'Pair of Bulls' and 'Best Six Head' was shown by Charles Osborn from Watkinsville, Georgia. In this show was heifers shown by Brad and Brian Shelnutt from Bishop, Georgia.

It was a good feeling for me to watch those I had introduced to

Shorthorns do well in a National Show. I wish to add the show facilities in Perry have now expanded and it is a world-class livestock venue.

The second pleasant experience I remember from this issue is on page 30 and is the Tennessee Beef Agribition that is held every year in Murfreesboro, Tennessee. I recall attending this event for several years. It is a great show-sale. I was able to see that year the Champion Bull, *B. W. Ace*, who was sired by *Trump* be purchased by Marvin Jackson from Dalton, Georgia to use in his commercial operation.

It was a great pleasure during the late 1960s and 1970s to attend the Polled Shorthorn Show and Sale in Cookeville, Tennessee. On page 6 of my March 1971 *Shorthorn World,* the Cookeville Sale is listed with 13 consignors, 60 head of cattle containing 17 bulls and 43 females. Mr. Don Smock of Whiteland, Indiana is listed as the Sales Manager and Mr. Charles Curtis is noted as the Secretary-Treasurer of the Tennessee Shorthorn Breeder's Association for that year. As a young, Southern Shorthorn breeder, these two show-sales gave me the opportunity to meet other Shorthorn breeders and purchase fine cattle for my herd. I also took several other new Georgia Shorthorn breeders to these events.

Since I mentioned *CCS Keystone* on page 73, I have also shown pictures of some of the very fine Shorthorns that he produced. I also mentioned that he was *HS Rodeo Drive 062WRX's* full brother. Dr. R. E. Hunsley, who at the time was the Executive Secretary of the American Shorthorn Association, wrote in the September 2001 issue of *Shorthorn Country* on page 15, "Farwell to a Shorthorn Legend." The last rites for *HS Rodeo Drive 062WRX* were delivered on July 3, 2001. Dr. Hunsley took a full page to list the outstanding contributions Rodeo made to the Shorthorn breed. he was crowned the 1988 National Shorthorn Bull at the North American in Louisville, Kentucky; a show that I got to see. When the opportunity came for me to purchase *CCS Keystone*, the full brother to Rodeo, I didn't hesitate. I can truly say that Keystone did the same as Rodeo for my Shorthorn herd. His best trait was his temperament. Dr. Hunsley stated that over the years, Rodeo Drive could be following a cow in heat and you could walk up to him in the pasture, scratch his back and he would literally follow you around to receive more attention. Keystone would do the same. This in itself is perhaps one of the three greatest attributes possessed by the Shorthorn breed today, "Disposition."

I have in my possession many copies of *Shorthorn World* and *Shorthorn Country* magazines. They have really helped me remember many great experiences I have had raising Shorthorns in Georgia for over 50 years. However, I have over the years placed these magazines in several Vo. Ag. classrooms as well as given new customers copies and encouraged them to subscribe to both publications. I also tried to keep a record of many of my customers over the years, to follow up with and help them get started with Shorthorns.

I have always been impressed with my results when I used the Irish strain and purchased cattle with the Irish strain blood when feasible at sales. The Alden Farms located in Hamilton, Missouri are a great family operation that did a very successful job using Irish Shorthorns. I kept a copy of their complete herd dispersion held on

November 27, 1993. First in their sale order were the offspring of *AF Shannon Margie 924*. She brought $71,000.00. Also is listed a picture of *AF RDS Margie 984* with calves. She was sired by *Deerpark Leader XVII* and her dam was *AF American Dream*, who was sired by *3W Payoff*. Still to this day I find this Irish blood, and thus the name, "K&M Irish Shorthorns."

There were 220 lots of cattle in that sale. Also, semen that went for $450-$500 a straw from *Deerpark Leader 13th Dividend*. He is the bull I mentioned that my Georgia livestock specialist saw in Kansas City and stated he was just a 'big bull.' I am glad I used the Irish Shorthorn influence in my herd.

GEORGIA SHORTHORNS
THE RED, WHITE, AND ROAN

MEMBERS   JUNIORS   EVENTS & ACTIVITIES   LINKS

2002-2003 GSA Officers and Directors

President	**Vice President**	**Secretary/Treasurer**
J.R. Boswell	Leonard Barrett	Joe Greene
PO Box 127	95 Sosby Road	3281 Brown Road
Maysville, GA 30558	Martin, GA 30557	Martin, GA 30557
706-652-2225	(706)384-7243	(706) 384-4877
Charles Osborn	Ken Parks	Thomas Bridges
2700 Greensboro Hwy	224 Bell Road	295 Bridges Road
Watkinsville, Ga 30677	Lula, GA 30529	Carnesville, GA 30521

Georgia Shorthorn Association Members
Please feel free to contact any of our members for infomation about Shorthorn cattle, or cattle for sale.

Chad & Tracy Barrett
C&T Farms
85 Gray Dove Trail
Dawsonville, GA 30534
ctbarrett@alltel.net

Kenneth & Marilyn Bridges
K & M Irish Polled
Shorthorns & Clubcalves
1030 Richard Bridges
Road
Commerce, GA 30530
(706) 757-3908

Greta & Shawn Collins
201 W. Mulberry Street
Moultrie, GA 31768

Dave Mooney
P.O. Box 614
Carnesville, GA 30521

Ken Parks
B.P. Shorthorns

Leonard Barrett
Lenbar Shorthorns
95 Sosby Road
Martin, GA 30557
(706) 384-7243
lwbarrett@hotmail.com

Thomas Bridges
Triple C Shorthorns
295 Bridges Road
Carnesville, GA 30521
(706) 335-5443
cccshorthorn@msn.com

Todd & Amy Edwards
970 RD 900
Fort Payne, AL 35967

David Mooney
1713 Akin Road
Carnesville, GA 30521
(706) 384-3959

Greg Walker

J.R. Boswell
B.P. Shorthorns
P.O. Box 127
Maysville, GA 30558
(706) 652-2225
bpshorthorn@alltel.net

Charles Campbell
Holly Creek Farm
914 Prince Beam Road
Chatsworth, GA 30705

Joe Greene

4G Farm
3281 Brown Road
Martin, GA 30557
(706) 384-4877
fourgfarm@alltel.net

Charles Osborn
Osborn Farm
2700 Greensboro Hwy.

5 Important Reasons To Use A Shorthorn Bull In A Commercial Cross Breeding Program

1. **Calving Ease** - 20 year USDA Research at Clay Center, Nebraska, Shorthorns were **Number One** in calving ease over all breeds.

2. **Milking Ability** – important for fast growing calves.

3. **Quality Grading Ability** - USDA Research - Shorthorn cross calves were number one to grade **Choice** at ideal market weights, (Top Dollar on new carcass price value market)

4. **Gentleness** - Easy to manage.

5. **New Genetics** for this area (Hybrid Vigor)

K & M Bridges Shorthorns
Telephone 706-768-3480

l to r: David Nixon, Star Bridges, Lisa Bridges, Marilyn Bridges, Kenneth Bridges

100 Cattlemen's Drive • P.O. Box 24510 • Macon, GA 31212-4510
(478) 474-6560 • Fax (478) 474-5732 • Web Site: www.gabeef.org

January 19, 2004

Kenneth R. Bridges
K & M Irish Polled Shorthorns
1030 Richard Bridges Road
Commerce, Georgia 30530

Dear Mr. Bridges:

I am very pleased to inform you that you have been selected as the Georgia Cattlemen's Association, "Purebred Cattleman of the Year." It was a close competition but your excellence in all aspects of purebred production prevailed. The committee was very impressed with the details of your operation.

The award will be presented on Saturday, February 14, at 6:30 p.m. at the GCA Annual Banquet in Athens. We would like to extend a special invitation to you and your family to join us for the evening. Please call the GCA office to confirm your attendance and the number of guests that you will be bringing and complimentary tickets will be waiting on you at the registration desk

Someone will be in touch with you in a couple of days to come over and make a video of your family and farm for the presentation to be shown at the convention.

Again, congratulations, and we look forward to seeing you at the convention.

Sincerely,

Michele Creamer

Michele Creamer
Business Manager

He's been called Mr. Shorthorn

Kenneth Bridges has worked diligently over the past 30+ years to develop Shorthorns in the state of Georgia and the southeast part of the United States.

by Debbie Hostert

For many years, Kenneth Bridges has utilized Shorthorn cattle in his ag education program. He sells or assists many of his students in purchasing Shorthorn heifers and buys them back after they are bred. Here, Kenneth instructs ag education student, Shawn Collins, in preparing his Shorthorn heifer for a Junior Shorthorn Show in Perry, Ga.

He's been called 'Mr. Shorthorn'. Another person stated 'if he ran for political office in the same manner and with the same enthusiasm as he has to promote the Shorthorn breed, no one could ever beat him.'

One thing is certain, Kenneth Bridges of Commerce, Ga., is a Shorthorn breeder and promoter through and through.

His love for the breed started during his first years as an ag teacher in the mountains of Georgia. Shorthorns were heavily used in the area.

"Typically the Shorthorns were big, roan cows that were good milkers and very gentle," Kenneth commented. "The cattle really impressed me."

Kenneth utilized Shorthorn cattle as projects for his students. He would work with his students, selling heifers to them and helping them buy Shorthorn heifers from other breeders. Then, he would help his students breed the heifers and, at times, also repurchase the heifers to develop his own herd. Many of his students over the years also started their own herds from their first project heifers. Bridges and his students had as many as 50 head of show cattle per year.

"Basically, if you expose them to your love of the cattle and get them working with the breed, that's the breed they will want," Kenneth comments quickly pointing out that ag teachers and extension agents are a great promotional venue. "If we promote the breed with them, the breed in that area will be strong," Kenneth added.

Bridges also sought out other venues to promote and develop the Shorthorn breed in his area.

"Cattlemen and juniors need an incentive to choose Shorthorns," Kenneth states. With this in mind, Bridges helped establish a $1,000 Champion and $500 Reserve Champion premium for the Shorthorn show at the Georgia Junior State Livestock Show. Hence, a large Shorthorn show was developed in an area where the number of Shorthorn herds was very low.

"My ag teacher peers always told me a Shorthorn steer would never win the Georgia Junior State Steer Show," Kenneth notes. "In 1992, a Shorthorn steer was named Grand Champion and won the event over 350 other steers."

Many people credit Kenneth Bridges for this accomplishment.

Bridges also helped start the Georgia Club Calf Producer, a program for breeders selling calves for show projects. Breeders purchase a tag and are included in a listing. Each breeder accumulates points with prizes awarded based on point totals.

In 1966, Kenneth and his first wife, Mary Ellen, started their cattle operation, K&M Irish Shorthorns, from a student's project. Kenneth and Mary Ellen had two children, Starling and Shannon. Mary Ellen passed away in 1978. Kenneth then married Marilyn, his current wife. She also had two children, David and Melanie.

"We purchased six females and one bull from one of my students. He was graduating and needed the money for his college education," Kenneth remembers. "The heifers were the old Scottish blood Shorthorns popular in the 50's and 60's. Scotch cattle were longer haired, smaller framed, very easy fleshing - the old style beef type."

The bull was a dual-purpose, registered bull tracing back to Meadow Lane Chieftain 2nd, coming from the Haumont herd, still in operation in Nebraska.

The Bridges built the herd by retaining heifers and purchasing other calves from Kenneth's students and through area sales.

Two bulls played a major role in developing their genetic base. The first was LTD Astronaut, a roan, horned, double-bred Deerpark Leader 13th, 'Dividend', son. He was sired by LSF Milestone, a Dividend son out of a Mandalong Super Flag daughter. Super Flag was the 1972 National Champion Bull. His dam was a JBS Astronaut show heifer purchased from Dale Wernicke.

"He produced lots of good brood cows for us," Kenneth comments adding they still have 15 of his daughters in their herd.

CCS Keystone * has also played a major role in the Bridges' herd. Keystone *, owned in partnership with Charles Osborn, is a red, horned, full brother to the infamous HS Rodeo Drive 062WR *x.

"He was a year younger, but I liked him better than Rodeo Drive *x," Kenneth states adding that Keystone * produced many show heifers including a Supreme Champion Over All Breeds.

Currently, Kenneth is using two bulls. FS RB Irish Breeze x is also owned in partnership with Charles Osborn and was purchased in a Combination Sale from Dr. Jim Freed. Maternally, he is line-bred AF 932 genetics and is sired by HFS HL Red Baron x, the sire of JG Red Cloud x, a past Reserve National Champion.

"We will also be using a really good bull called 'Tom', Kenneth states. "He is a 'CD' son out of a 3W Payoff daughter."

'CD' also sired the popular CF

The Bridges Family

Kenneth Bridges was married to the former Mary Ellen Davis, who passed away in 1978. He and Mary Ellen had two children, Starling Kenneth Bridges, a prominent psychotherapist and addiction specialist in Helen, Georgia, and Shannon Marella Bridges Lay, a talented and loving wife, mother, and businesswoman, who passed away in 2016.

Bridges is now married to the former Marilyn Nixon, and they have two children, David and Melanie. Marilyn is a graduate of Berea College, Berea, Ky., and is a registered nurse. David Nixon is a CDL Commercial truck driver and manager and operator of K&M Shorthorn Cattle of Commerce, Ga. Melanie Critelli is manager of a major graphic arts company in Atlanta.

Bridges' faith holds a prominent place in his life, and he and Marilyn are members of First Baptist Church of Commerce, Ga. He has served as a deacon in several Baptist churches.

Bridges' grandchildren include Garnette Gravel, an attorney from Atlanta; Mendi and Drew Lay of Watkinsville, Georgia, who are both college students; and Reilly Mahon of Charlotte, who is a logistics coordinator for J.B. Hunt Trucking Company.

Made in the USA
Columbia, SC
21 September 2020